FUNCTIONING OF AUTONOMOUS DISTRICT COUNCILS IN MEGHALAYA

FUNCTIONING OF AUTONOMOUS DISTRICT COUNCILS IN MEGHALAYA

Sujit Kumar Dutta

AKANSHA PUBLISHING HOUSE
New Delhi-110 002 (India)

AKANSHA PUBLISHING HOUSE
4649-B/21 Ansari Road, Darya Ganj,
New Delhi-110002 (INDIA)
Phone : 9811582579/011-23263193
Email : ektabooks@yahoo.com

Functioning of Autonomous District Councils in Meghalaya First Published 2002
Reprint 2026

ISBN 81-87606-13-4

PRINTED IN INDIA

Published by M.P. Misra for Akansha Publishing House,

Contents

Preface

Functioning of Autonomous District Council in Meghalaya is the burning question of the day. However, any person who wants to understand the problem by asking the functionaries of District Councils of Meghalaya about its status may get a very rosy picture. From the available detailed-recorded account of the functioning of District Councils one might have an idea that District Council has been functioning as well as any other existing local government in the country. But this seems to me paradoxical as the empirical findings show that the existing District Council in Meghalaya is not at all fulfilling the local needs; rather it seems to have been created to fulfil the interest of a few affluent people and not for the welfare or benefit of the mass as pointed out by a good number of traditional Khasi Chiefs. In fact it is an institution which has created more factional conflicts and cleavages within the Khasi Society today. Hence, the creation of District Council is a controversial issue in Meghalaya. Much analysis is done and presented in the text. The study presents numerous recommendations and suggestions to make District Council a true representative local government by resolving the disputes and conflicts with the grass root level institutions and discontentment of the true functionaries at the grass root level.

The author is indebted to those chiefs who gave the true information and unveiled the truth. He is also indebted to Dr. B.K. Thapliyal, Director, NIRD-NERC for his encouragement and suggestion right from the grounding stage of the project. I want to thank those who helped with editing and advice: Prof. Abu Naser Ahmed, Director, OKD Institute of Social change & Development, Guwahati, for commenting on an early draft and Prof. A.C.Talukdar, Dean of Social Science Arunachal University, who has read and wisely critiqued many of the drafts.

The author is also thankful to his two research investigators namely, Ms. Jhimly Barua and Sri Mukta Ram Deka who took pains to collect some critical information, and Mr John F.Kharshiing (a thinker on the Local Government issues in Meghalaya) who supplied some valuable documents. Their association with the project, though short, was meaningful.

Last but not the least the author is grateful to Mr. I.K. Bania, who took the trouble to check the entire write-up, Mr B.S. Dobal who helped me in sketching the map of the Khasi States and Non – States and Mr A.Rahman for taking pains in typing the often difficult manuscripts.

NIRD-NERC, Guwahati

Sujit Kumar Dutta
Dy. Director

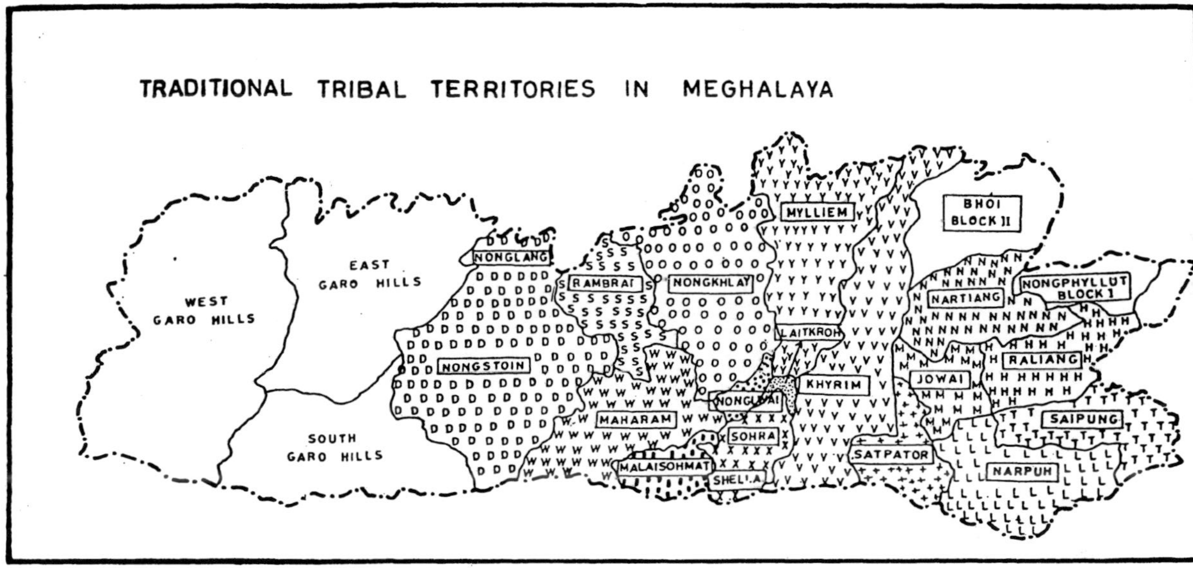

The following Zones are occupied by the Khasi Chiefs – *Syiems, Lyngdohs, Wahadadar and Sirdar:*

DDDDDD SSSSSS YYYYYY WWWWWW XXXXXX VVVVVV OOOOOO
,.... •••••• ||||||

The following Zones are Occupied by the Dollois of the Jaintia Hills.:

NNNNNN HHHHHH LLLLLL +++++++ TTTTTT MMMM

1

Introduction

Survival of the traditional institutions of Khasi Hills of Meghalaya is the question of the day. The struggle is more to prove the strength through fraudulent method on one hand while on the other a section of Khasi elites are desperately trying to crucify the traditional institutions in the name of so called reforms and progress. This is the general remark of most of the Khasi States Chiefs. However, it has become imperative to understand the discontentment of these Chiefs first rather than to understand the local government's functional role. The District Council today stands on a plank with the support of the Sixth Schedule of the Constitution. The drafting committee of the Constitution also comprised persons like Rev. Nicholas Roy, Rup Nath Brahma, Kuladhar Chaliha and Rohini Kumar Choudhury who were also closely associated with the Bordoloi Committee. The master of making the draft of the Sixth Schedule was late G.N. Bordoloi. Bordoloi Committee's recommendations however, did not say anything about the future status and position of 25 Khasis States except advocating the Sixth Schedule. Hence, the Chiefs of the Khasi States felt ignored. In fact immediately after the independence, the necessity of enlarging the content of the accession of the Khasi States was more acutely felt by the Ministry of States. The then Governor of Assam and the Agent to the Dominion of India including his assistant had to utilise all their diplomatic resources to convince the standing committee of the Federation of Khasi States[1] to enlarge the scope of the Instrument of

Accession. The rulers of the Khasi states ultimately agreed to sign a new Instrument of Accession along with the Annexed Agreement. It was on December 15, 1947, that nineteen[2] out of the twenty-five rulers signed the Instrument of Accession. The other six states, however, expressed their inability to sign the same without the consent of their state ***Darbars***. The main reason for not signing the merger agreement initially was that the rulers of the Khasi states were not Zamindars as they were not owners of the land. They were merely elected heads but cannot claim any right of control over the land (Lyngdoh, 1996:25). It is interesting to note that both the Khasi hills and the Jaintia hills land never belong to the Chiefs, ***Syiem*** or ***Rajas***. Naturally the Jaintia **Raja** could not impose any tax on the land of the ***pnars***, and the ***Syiems*** or other heads can not levy taxes on the Khasi people for the use of the land (Pugh, n.d :32). These six states ultimately could not escape but had to sign the Instrument of Accession due to the persistent negotiation from the Dominion Agent and his party.

By this instrument, the Chiefs acceded to India. Accordingly all existing administrative arrangements were made. The position continued till the institution came into force; the Chiefs lost whatever administrative power they had by the merger of these 25 states in Assam and the governance of these states began to be carried on henceforth according to the provisions of the Sixth Schedule.(Cajee, 1960) Naturally, the Khasi States did not get a place in the purview of the Sixth Schedule. Even the drafting committee did not consult Dr. G.S. Guha who was the representative of the Khasi in the Constituent Assembly. As a result the Khasi States with long persuasions with the Ministry of States came with an agreement that the future position of the Khasi States should be decided by the Khasi States themselves in close association with the Dominion Agent. The Dominion Agent demanded a constitution-making ***Darbar*** of the Khasi States consisting of all the heads of the Khasi States and other members elected by the people. ***Darbar*** was also to have power to nominate some members. The Dominion Agent framed rules for the election.

The first election to the constitution-making ***Darbar*** of the Khasi States was held during December 1948. This ***Darbar*** consisted of 89 members – 25 heads of the States, 56 elected and 8 nominated members. It was inaugurated by the then Governor of Assam who thanked the rulers of the Khasi States for having signed the Instrument of Accession and Standstill Agreement. He also indicated the possibility of including the Khasi States within the purview of the Sixth Schedule of the Draft Constitution.

The second session of the ***Darbar*** was held on May 16, 1949, where Dr. H. Lyngdoh and Prof. R.R. Thomas were elected as Chairman and Vice-Chairman of the ***Darbar.*** Jor Manik Syiem, the Secretary of the Federation of the Khasi States was elected secretary of this ***Darbar.***

Meanwhile A. Alley, member of The Draft Constitution Committee of The Sixth Schedule initially intended to move the resolution before the Assam Government to allot at least 5 seats for the District of Khasi and Jaintia Hills including the Khasi States and one more seat for the Town of Shillong in the Assam Legislative Assembly and also to take steps to prepare electoral rolls for the people in the Khasi States. A. Alley ultimately did not move the resolution as he felt that the resolution prepared by Rev. Nichols Roy was according to him, a better one.

The main issue that came up for discussion in the 3rd session of the Khasi States Constitution-Making ***Darbar*** was to introduce a united administration for the State and non-State Areas of Khasi and Jaintia Hills as advocated by Nichols Roy in view of the fact that the people of the district belonged to the same Khasi race.

In fact they wanted to establish a separate statusquo on one hand and to bind the society together with traditional values on the other. Properties were undivided and maintained by the community or individual, and the traditional heads such as ***Syiem, Lyngdoh, Sirdar or Wahadadar*** were the custodian of these lands and property of those people who live under this jurisdiction. These bodies are apolitical, but for survival they formed Federation of Khasi States and the non-states, which was established in 1933.

Now the question arises whether this plank (based on Sixth Schedule) is a sufficient condition to sustain those traditional institutions or not? Thinkers, administrators, scholars have diverse opinions regarding the provision of Autonomous District Councils in the Constitution. Some of their views are:

Kuladhar Chaliha, Rajeswar Prasad and Rohini Kumar Choudhury gave opinion against the formation of Autonomous District Councils. Mr. Chaliha feels that "we still have British Mentality – a separatist tendency to keep them (the tribals) away. In future it will be a Tribalstan, just like Pakistan". Rajeswar Prasad opined that they would lead to the establishment of another Pakistan in this country. He is a staunch believer of Unitary State. But Rohini Kumar Choudhury is a staunch protagonist of the policy of assimilation. Hence, he advocates the assimilation of Tribal and Non-Tribal (Constitution Assembly Debate, n.d:1008).

However, Nichols Ray, Gopinath Bordoloi, Lakshminarayan Sahu, A.V. Thakkar and Jaipal Singh supported the formation of District Councils and therefore supported the spirit of the Sixth Schedule. The only argument these people have is that the hill people will not only be safeguarded by this Sixth Schedule, but it will satisfy hill people in many ways and they will be able to come closer to the rest of the country.

In fact those who are in favour of the of assimilation want to assimilate the tribal people by force. Naturally they hold an imperialist attitude and suffer from superiority complex. They failed to see the distinction between integration and assimilation. In fact assimilation involves total loss of cultural identity of the group as a result of its complete absorption into the dominant group. Instead of assimilation, integration must be encouraged.

However, the arguments advanced by Dr. B.R. Ambedkar were so realistic that the Constituent Assembly understood the full justification for the creation of the District Councils (*Ibid*).

The age-old rivalry between the traditional institutions (Khasi States and non-states) and the Autonomous District Council created under the Sixth Schedule is well known. Even today it is eluding a solution. At times distrust attitudes among them lead to conflict. In such circumstances the autonomy of the tribal institutions is jeopardised and the struggle sustained. This is the turmoil within the Khasi society and their institutions today. Most of the Chiefs feel that they are now under the control of District Councils. By enquiry it has been found that all the Chiefs are now under the jurisdiction of District Councils. The District Councils under the Act of 1959 wholly regulate the succession and appointment of Chiefs and headmen (Appointment of Succession of Chief Act). The Supreme Court of India observed in 1960 that *Syiem* was a functionary under the District Council. All the Chiefs were now presiding officers of the Additional Subordinate District Council Courts. But their decisions are subject to appellate jurisdiction of the Subordinate District Council Court at Shillong. As regards financial matters, the Chiefs pay one-eighth of the total income to the District Council. The Council has also certain control over the budget of the Chiefs. Overall it has been found that the Chiefs are today under hard pressure in many ways; even their status has become subordinate. In such a situation many of them have become aggressive and are preparing for a revolt.

Forty-seven years have passed since the time when the autonomous district councils were established under the framework of the Sixth Schedule of the Constitution, but no sincere attempts have so far been made to have a full-ranged in-depth study of the traditional institutions. Many legislations have been enacted, but instead of improving them, these legislations seem to have come into direct confrontation with the well-established customary laws and practices which are attached to the existing traditional institutions. At present these institutions are in need of a positive dynamic leadership which possesses a sense of balance and proportion coupled with a sense of direction. It is easy to destroy whatever they have in their possession rather than to preserve the best and to make progressive improvement upon them; it is just impossible to re-build and reconstruct any good thing, which they have destroyed. The need of the hour, they feel, is wisdom and political sagacity to pave the way for the future generations. This is what some very aggrieved chiefs of the Khasi States have felt.

In spite of all these the traditional Khasi political structure still prevails in Meghalaya, though with the advent of the British rule and the promulgation of the Constitution of India later it has undergone modification to a certain extent. But District Councils have weakened the function of tribal courts in Meghalaya so much so that the Khasi states have virtually come under the domination of the state officials as well as the District Councils. Naturally the Khasi states have come to occupy the subordinate position.

The basic differences between the British administration and the Independent India in dealing with the Khasis are:

i. While dealing with the Khasis the British administration did not interfere in the tribal customs and laws. The judicial powers of the *Syiem* and traditional political authority were curtailed only to a limited extent. As against this the establishment of District Council court after independence has eroded the Chief's judicial powers to a considerable extent.

ii. The overall impact of the British rule was that although the *Syiem* and his *Myntries* and other officials remained in their offices, they were divested of their real power which was then vested in the Deputy Commissioner. At present the authority structure is organised at the level of District Council, Deputy Commissioner (only in certain Khasi area of the city) and finally the High Court.

However, the *Syiem* as the chief of the tribe, is always respected. He still receives different forms of tributes from his people. Despite the erosion of his powers and rights, he still plays a vital role in the administrative affairs of the tribe. He supervises the conduct of his subordinate authorities at the *raid* and village level. If a village headman or a commune headman is found incompetent and charged with abusing his powers, the *Syiem* can order fresh elections in order to replace him. He still protects the rights of the people, administers justice and punishes the culprits. After the formation of District Councils all *Syiems* have been given the powers of Additional Magistrates in their respective *Syiemships*. Accordingly they are empowered to try civil and criminal cases except murder case.

The present study focuses mainly on this aspect as stated. The approach taken to study the different institutions exiting within these communities is very systematic and new. The study would find out the reasons behind their problems of existence and non-sustenance as an institution of self-government. Finally it will try to know why these institutions are not taken into confidence so as to involve them in the development work of the state, which is a debatable and controversial issue of the day.

2

The Existence and Functioning of ADC in Meghalaya

The existence of Autonomous District Council was obviously not the choice of Khasi people in Meghalaya. In fact it was at the cabinet mission's advice that the Constituent Assembly of India set up an advisory committee on January 24, 1947 regarding the formation of Autonomous District Councils. The committee later on constituted two sub-committees on February 27, 1947, namely the North-East Frontier (Assam) Tribal and Excluded Areas Sub-Committee; and the other is known as the Excluded and Partially Excluded Areas (other than Assam) Sub-Committee. Sri Gopinath Bordoloi was the Chairman of the North - East Frontier (Assam) Tribal and Excluded Areas Sub-Committee; so it is known as Bordoloi Committee. This Committee studied the administrative set-up carefully in the hill areas including Khasi hills with a view to building up an autonomous body in the administration of the hills so that the tribal people could continue to follow their traditional life. The Bordoloi Committee recommended the setting up of the administration of tribal areas, based on the concept of regional autonomy in all matters affecting their customs, laws of inheritance as well as administration of justice, land, forest etc. The sub-committee's report was submitted on July 28, 19473.

The Constituent Assembly accepted the recommendations of Bordoloi Committee and incorporated them in the Sixth

Schedule(Dutta, 1998:58). By the Act 1935, the Tribal Areas in Assam were kept as 'Excluded Areas' in the Constitution of India, 1950, and provision was made for the constitution of Autonomous District councils[4]. This was done in such a way that the tribal people could be in a position to enjoy some rights of self-government for socio-economic development and preservation of ethnic identities. This arrangement did not come in the way of formation of separate states. The relevance of district councils to social development of the tribals was not ignored as it is evident from the fact that even within the tribal State of Meghalaya and the Union Territory of Mizoram district councils have been functioning. There are of course differences of opinion about the need for retaining the district councils in these states (Ganguly, 1988). However, six Tribal Districts of Assam were included under the Autonomous Districts under the Sixth Schedule. The controversies/differences of opinion regarding the retention of district council in Meghalaya are yet to be clarified. But the remark of Baljied *Syiem* is worth mentioning. In his opinion JJM Nichols Roy did not go out to protect the rights of the Khasi people. Ultimately there came out the Sixth Schedule, which was actually imposed without taking the public opinion or existing local institutions in to consideration. District Council is a political institution which, though meant to be the protector of traditions and customs of the Khasis, has actually been so much politicised that it only serves the interests of some elected members. Actually, people do not look to the council so much for protection of the traditions of the society as for some measly grants which ultimately end up in a few pockets. It is the political leaders both from the district councils and the state government who have not really been sincere in their duties towards their community. He felt that most of the problems could be solved if district council was scrapped. It is the duty of the state government to see that a new legislation comes out to ensure that the traditional institutions are left unhindered to co-exist healthily. For him the traditional institutions have some limitations in modern society Even they are open to changes, but they should have the right to choose the changes required. They are in need of a healthy tradition and good political leaders who are not selfish and who really work for the benefit and development of modern society (Syiem, 1988).

The Sixth Schedule was designed to confer a considerable amount of autonomy on the tribal people by giving them protection to retain their identity according to their own genius politically, socially and economically through their elected representatives and nominated members. The Sixth Schedule provides a type of local governmental arrangement, which aims to better the life of the tribal people, keeping in view the ample opportunity to grow in their own roots (Jyrwa, n.d).

In reality, the spirit of the Sixth Schedule is to provide complete safeguards to the tribal communities in respect of land, forest, and system of justice and social customs. It was felt that the state and central government would help them in securing the benefits of a democratic, progressive and liberal administration. In order to achieve these aims the constitution has given the power to make laws on various subjects applicable to the tribal people as enshrined in the Sixth Schedule (Bose, 1979:182 – 184).

Against this backdrop, the District Councils/Autonomous Local Government came into being in Tribal Areas of the North-Eastern Region especially to introduce internal autonomy in tribal compact areas for protecting the social, economic and cultural interests of the tribal population. It has been felt that the Autonomous District Councils should be set up in terms of the Fifth Schedule of the Constitution. Accordingly the Tribal Areas Autonomous District Council Bill/Act was passed by the Legislative Assemblies of the respective states. There are instances of the Sixth Schedule being introduced by the Central Government but with the concurrence of the state governments thereby restricting the outsiders to enter those states freely until and unless they possess inner-line permits.

As regards the composition of District Councils, it varied from time to time. In 1952, the District Council consisted of 24 members, 18 elected and six nominated. When the government nominated non-tribals, the Khasi protested and the nomination element was completely abolished. But the Jaintia Hills Council continues to have the system of nomination. In 1971 when the Sixth Schedule was amended, the strength of the District Council was fixed at 30 including four nominated members. At present the Khasi Hills Autonomous District Council is divided into 29 constituencies, the Jaintia Hills into 16 constituencies. The number of nominated members is one in the Khasi Hills and three in the Jaintia Hills. The total strength of the Jaintia Hills is 19.

All the activities to be undertaken by the Khasi Hills Autonomous District Council (KHADC) are outlined in the sixth scheduled of the Indian Constitution. The major activities are:

i. Activities based on forest which are mostly managed by the ADC.

ii. The ADC looks after matters pertaining to primary education (lower primary) which involves looking after the activities of the primary schools, their administration, day to day activities, payments of teachers etc.

iii. Taxation, i.e., professional taxes are to be paid by all professionals including businessmen and government employees to the ADC.

iv. The council looks after activities involving fisheries.

v. Another major activity of the council is public works. This involves building of roads, bridges, pavements, footpaths, digging of ponds etc.

vi. Elaka administration which involves an overall charge of the traditional Khasi organisations.

vii. Trade and Commerce.

viii. Market regulation.

ix. Transport.

x. Control of grazing grounds.

xi. Control over land resources.

Basic Functions of the KHADC:

There are three basic functions of the ADC:

i. **Legislative:**

The district council, as per the provisions of the Sixth Schedule to the constitution, has to enact laws and regulations as well as frame rules for implementing them. Such laws and regulations have to be placed before the council's session in the form of bills for consideration. After the Council passes the bills they are sent to the government for concurrence. The existing list of subjects on which the District Council can legislate covers all the important social and personal aspects of tribal life.

ii. Executive:

The executive functions of the District Council are vested in the executive committee. Each member of the Executive Committee is entrusted with specific subjects and the Chief Executive Member (CEM) makes the allocation of the subjects to the members. The Council can discharge some functions in exercise of its executive powers even before the relevant laws are passed provided these are within the purview of the Sixth Schedule. At the highest level, all executive functions of the District Council are vested in the Executive Committee headed by the CEM who is elected by the members of the council from among themselves. The executive committee disposes of all matters of administration of the district except those that involve any important change in the administrative system of the autonomous district.

The Executive Committee is collectively responsible to the council for all executive orders, policy matters and their exception. It frames the policies, prepares the budget, executes them and mostly initiates legislation in the council. The Executive Committee has a secretary who controls and supervises the various branches of the council and is in the immediate charge of the day–to–day administration. Thus, it has separate branches for general administration, land revenue, forests, civil works, education, rural development, transport, taxation, and relief and rehabilitation, besides the legislative and judicial branches.

iii. Judiciary:

Paragraph 4 of the Sixth Schedule empowers the District Council to constitute village courts for the trial of suits and cases in which both parties are members of the Schedule Tribes. It may appoint suitable persons as members of such village councils or presiding officers of such courts as may be necessary for the execution of laws made by the District Council. According to the amendments of the Sixth Schedule under the Act, the Governor is authorised to make rules for regulating the constitution of the village councils and courts and the power to be exercised by them.

All the three ADCs have constituted their courts of appeals. Each has a judge and a magistrate. The traditional courts of the chiefs have always been functioning as additional subordinate courts of the District Council with the traditional chiefs as presiding officers.

Entrusted Functions:

Apart from the basic functions as already mentioned, the ADCs have some entrusted functions. However, the state Government is not authorised to entrust any of its powers to the District Council. In order to retain both the Mikir and the N.C. Hills, the Government of Assam made several costly promises like transfer of more functions and powers together with necessary finance and personnel. Hence, paragraph 6 of the Sixth Schedule was amended whereby it is provided that the Governor may entrust either conditionally or unconditionally some functions to the District Councils. The functions enumerated are agriculture, animal husbandry, community projects, cooperative societies, social welfare, village planning or any other matter which the executive power of the State extends. But the Governor of Meghalaya has entrusted none of these subjects to any of the District Councils.

Source of Funds of ADC:

There are some major sources of funds of the ADC, which are listed below:

i. Land, which abounds in major minerals (coal, silimonites, lime stone etc.) and minor minerals (sand, pebbles etc.). The ADC gets its share of income from these resources from the state government.

ii. Income of the ADC from the taxes collected at the toll gates.

iii. Share of income from trade and commerce.

iv. Income from professional taxes.

v. Revenue from forests.

Constraint of the District Councils Today:

The Autonomous District Councils in Meghalaya are facing the following constraints:

(i) There is resource (Financial) crunch. Moreover, the resources provided under the Sixth Schedule such as the power to collect taxes on land and building, and tolls on person resident in the District could not be made use of an account of the tradition and customs prevailing in the District.

ii. ADC has been given powers to collect taxes but not for the collection of royalties and fees on subjects within its legislative and administrative competence (paragraph 3 as per Supreme Court judgement in Civil appeal Nos. 2069 –70 of 1972). The revenue resources of the council will be augmented if these powers are given to the ADCs.

(iii) The share of royalty in respect of any area within the District Council between District Council and the State Government as agreed upon was 60:40 ratio (e.g. , share of royalty on coal). A dispute arose later on and the case was referred to the Governor whose determined the share as 25:75 between the District Council and the State Government.

(iv) Assent or approval of the Governor to the Bills passed by the ADC is often accorded after a considerable period of time, say two years or even more. This defeats the very purpose of the Bills and the Council is not in a position to implement its intention to promote good administration on different subjects.

(v) Paragraph 14 empowers the Governor to appoint a commission to enquire into the administration of a District council or any particular matters specified by him relating to the administration of the Autonomous District in the State. The Central Government had been given any power to the ADC to implement their schemes directly.

(vi) Shares on royalty on major and minor minerals, taxes on vehicles collected by the State Government constitute one of the major resources of the council. The State

Government instead of paying the share in full and in time adopted a policy to release the share in the form of advance, and sometimes to deduct from such share Election expenses and other charges incurred by it from time to time without consent of the council. Above all no account pertaining to the actual collection and the share due to the council was ever made available to the council.

(vii) Fund for carrying out developmental activities as provided according to the present system are found to be inadequate as well as unworkable. To meet the basic need of the people sufficient funds have also to be released from the Council's own fund. During 1997-98 Rs.90 lakhs was provided for this purpose from the account of JHADC, whereas the state released only Rs. 57,40,510 for the purpose of Council's own plan, building and rural communication including implementation of forest schemes, strengthening of staff and salary to the deputed staff. Hence, it has been observed that the funds released as grants-in-aid are far from being sufficient to meet the actual requirement of the council. Allocation of funds needs to be enhanced substantially.

(viii) There is no provision in the Sixth Schedule for the State Police to act at the instant of District Council and therefore enforcement of the council orders etc. has become a major handicap in the council's day to day administration. The council has been given the power to constitute village or town police under clause (f) of sub-paragraph (I) of paragraph 3 of the Schedule. However, in view of the meager resources of the council, it is not possible to create such a force. It is also obligatory on the part of the ADC to organise and strengthen the traditional Institution, but for paucity of fund no significant improvement could be made so far on this behalf.

(ix) When Meghalaya was created, the councils in Meghalaya were subjected to great financial constraints. This is due to the fact that funds provided earlier under article 275 are no longer available, with the result that the Management of Primary Education – as the first casualty – had to be taken over temporarily by the state government and it is continuing till date even after about 10 years.

(x) By the 73rd/74th amendment to the constitution in 1993, substantial administrative and financial powers have been delegated to local bodies constituted all over the country (where PR system is existing), but the Sixth Schedule does not provide for devolution of development powers to ADCs/Autonomous councils. As a result financial and administrative autonomy of local bodies in other parts of the country has become much greater than that in schedule areas.

3

Methodology

Information was generated through questionnaire as well as personnal contact with the functionaries of both the District Councils under study. As the district administration is not at all involved or interested in the District Council's affairs we did not get much information from them. For this very reason they were not consulted very intensively. The very purpose of the study delimits us to consult the functionaries of the two District Councils, namely, the Khasi Hills Autonomous District Council (KHADC) and the Jaintia Hills Autonomous District Councils (JHADC). The former is comprised of three Districts (East Khasi Hills, West Khasi Hills and Ri-bhoi), and the latter consists of a single district. Our representative samples were chosen accordingly. Further, the District Councils feel that the age-old traditional institutions, which have existed and spread over the territory under these District Councils, may also be included in our study. Hence, samples were also taken from among these institutions. The representative samples are taken from the Chiefs of these institutions and the territories they occupy that are known as *elaka*/or *Hima* as the Khasi people term it. The Chiefs of these ***Hima*** are known as ***Hima – Chief***. These Chiefs are having different names in different places, such as ***Hima Syiems, Lyngdoh, Sirdar, Wahadadar*** and their territory is known as ***Hima*** but ***Dolloi*** areas are known as ***Elaka***. The entire ***Hima/ elaka*** are clubbed into 16 zones based on their geographical proximity and social groupings. Our representative samples were taken from among the Chiefs of the ***Himal elaka***. Since the functioning of all the Chiefs is not of similar type, so the sample were taken from different zones. Further, some of these Chiefs' area is quite large, and therefore, for their operational convenience, more villages under their ***elaka*** form a commune and they are known as ***Syiem raid (Raij)***. And the ***Lyngdoh*** area is known as ***Lyngdoh raid*** similarly. Therefore, samples were also taken from the Chiefs of these ***raids***. However, in the case of the Jaintia Hills, there is no complication as they have only one system, i.e., the ***Dollois*** who are the ***elaka*** Chiefs of their respective area and their style of functioning is same throughout the district.

The ***Syiems, Lyngdoh, Wahadadar, Sirdar*** and ***Dollois*** were interviewed separately to get their diverse opinions. Similarly, from the grass-root levels, we collected information from a few representative village headmen.

For secondary source of data, we consulted and collected materials from the District Councils as well as some written documents from ***Syiem Durbar's*** Office. However, a good deal of materials were also collected from one of the freelance consultants of the ***Syiems***.

Primary Data Collection:

For this purpose we use the multistage stratified sampling method. The first stage unit was the District Council, the second stage the ***elaka*** (***Hima***), the third stage unit the commune (***raid***) and the fourth stage unit the village ***darbar***. Out of the seven districts four districts were selected. Out of 25 ***elaka*** of Khasi states 9 were consulted and 4 samples were taken from the grass-root levels (village ***darbar***) i.e, the village headmen.

The required data were generated from each of those functionaries with the aid of specially structured pre-tested questionnaire. Field visits were made for pre-testing the questionnaire whereas the final data were collected by staying in the field.

Sample Design:

Representative Samples at the District Council's Level

Districts	Name of the District Councils	Respondents
East Khasi Hills → West Khasi Hills → Ri-bhoi →	Khasi Hills Autonomous District Councils (KHADC)	Chief Executive Member One MDC Secretary District Council
Jaintia Hills	Jaintia Hills Autonomous District Councils (JHADC)	Chief Executive Member One MDC Secretary District Council

Representative Samples at the Khasi States and non-States Level

District	*Syiem-ship*	*Wahada-dar-ship*	*Sirdar-ship*	*Lyngdoh-*	*Dolloiship*
East Khasi Hills*	3	1	–	1	–
West Khasi Hills*	1	–	–	–	–
Ri-bhoi*	–	–	1	–	–
Jaintia Hills (non–state)**	–	–	–	–	2

* There are 25 Khasi States in Meghalaya.
** Non – States areas include 31 Sirdarships in the Khasi Hills and Jowai Sub – division in the Khasi and Jaintia Hills.

Representative Samples at the Commune Level Sardarship (Raid Sardar)

District	Respondents
East Khasi Hills	1
West Khasi Hills	Not available
Ri-bhoi	1
Jaintia Hills	Not applicable

Representative Samples at the Grassroot level (Village Darbar)

Districts	Respondents (Village Headmen)
East Khasi Hills	1
West Khasi Hills	1
Ri-bhoi	1
Jaintia Hills	1

Analysis of Data:

The data were generated for the purpose of this study through the sample design as mentioned. The analysis of data was done mainly to find out about the functioning of the institution at the district level, but there is no denying the fact that the study also tries to find out the organic linkage between the other lower bodies of the same institution. Discussions were also held with the functionaries of other lower bodies. Interestingly, it has been found that these institutions are functioning at the submerged level, so their actual functioning required in-depth analysis. And accordingly it was done.

Tools and Techniques:

Since the nature of data is mostly of descriptive and historical nature, hence, content analysis is the only technique applied. However cross verification was done as per the requirement.

Period of Study:

Duration of this study is very short, April – May 2000 as the study is short term one. The period being a very busy time for those functionaries (the sample respondents), naturally we had to complete the work very hurriedly.

Constraint of Data Collection:

1. Both the ADCs are short lived, and the bodies get frequently dissolved and suffer from instability. It has

been seen that during the period of our study both the ADCs faced no confidence motion; one still remains under the control of an administrative officer deputed by the Governor. Hence, it was difficult to get information from the functionaries of District Councils. However it was managed through long persuasion.

2. Most of the *Hima* Chiefs were reluctant to interact straightway because they are quite suspicious about outsiders. Ultimately we had to reach them through local influential persons.

3. Most of the Chiefs at the *elaka* level have been suffering from their status, and they have been organising themselves to fightfor their right of their own *elaka*. In this regard they do not want to share their views with the outsider. Hence, it was very difficult to get information easily.

4. At the commune/*raid* level, the chief is known as *raid sardar*. They are generally heads of two to three villages. They are working under some *syiems/ lyngdohs* etc. But some of these *sardars* do not agree to stay under the control of their *syiems/ lyngdoh*. Hence, they function like self styled *Sardar*. For their sustenance they keep link with District Council and Government. We wanted to get one such sample for our study, but he was reluctant to reply to our questions.

5. At the village *Darbar* level we did not face problem at all in getting information. They are liberal to all, and this is precisely because they get help from every body. Even the state government engaged them for development work. But as their relationship with their chiefs is very intrinsic they find it difficult to differentiate between their relationship with the chiefs and that with Government and ADC.

4

Set Up of Khasi States and Non-States

25 Khasi States (Menon, 1997:310–311) have been classified into four types: one presided over by *Syiems,* though taken from one family are appointed by election, the second presided over by *Wahadadar,* the third by *Sirdars* and the fourth by *Lyngdoh*. These offices are entirely elective. The election of *Syiems* and the others was subject to confirmation by the British Government (Administrative Report of Khasi – Jaintia Hills, 1976). From 1952 onwards, this power has rested with the Khasi Hills District Council. (Bhattacharya, 1985:52). But with the coming into force of the Constitution of India the Khasi States were merged with the State of Assam by the Constitution itself without through any instrument of Merger as was done in respect of similar States in other parts of India. In spite of the creation of the ADC under the Sixth Schedule to Constitution, the tribal Chiefs with their respective *Darbars* have continued to collect excise revenue, land revenue, forest revenue, and tolls and rents from their own markets and *haats* etc. With the revenue so collected they run and manage their own administration (Instrument of Accession, 1948). Constitution making *Darbar* of the Khasi States felt that the Sixth Schedule did not guarantee the traditional rights and privileges of the Khasi people. Hence, the *Darbar* further proposes the following amendments of the Constitution of India:

i. The Federation of Khasi states established since 1933 be given due recognition by including the 25 Khasi states and the non-states Areas (31 ***Sirdarships*** in the Khasi Hills and the Jowai Sub-Division in the Khasi and Jaintia Hills) in the First Schedule of the constitution.

ii. Nothing in this Constitution shall be construed as empowering any authority to make laws or to exercise its powers or to undermine the democratic institutions and the traditional customs and usages of the Khasis, nor to diminish their traditional rights and privileges and shall correspond to matters specified in the annexed Agreement of the Instrument of Accession, signed by the Khasi States and accepted by the Governor General of India on the 17th August 1948 (The letter of the Chairman, Constitution Making Darbar, 1948).

It is clear from their memorandum that the people in the states wished to preserve traditions and customs. And they were anxious to maintain their autonomy as far as possible, and were opposed to the idea of outright merger with Assam.The Govt. of India ultimately decided that the District Councils in the tribal areas should be given a large measure of autonomy. Detailed and specific provisions for the governance of the Khasi Hill States and other tribal areas of Assam were included in the Sixth Schedule to the Constitution.(Menon, *op.cit.;* Lyngdoh, *op.cit.*). This is where the confusion arose. In fact the Bordoloi Committee merely made a pssing reference about the position of the Khasi states. It did not make any recommendation that the Khasi states should come within the purview of the District Council(Lyngdoh, *Ibid.,* 208). Even the representation of members from the Khasi and the Jaintia Hills was not adequate. According to the report of the Bordoloi Committee, the population of the Khasi and the Jaintia Hills was 105463 but that was the population of only the British portion of the Khasi and the Jaintia Hills(Lyngdoh, *Ibid.*). Between August 1947 and February 1948 the process of accession of the Khasi

States to the Indian Union was completed. A long debate took place in the Constituent Assembly on the question of determining the future status of these Khasi States. When the Constitution of India was finally adopted on 29th November 1949, we find that these states were put under the purview and framework of the Sixth Schedule of the Constitution of India. It is clearly mentioned here that Khasi polity and democracy has a three-tier system with built-in-checks and balance. At the bottom there is a village (Village ***Darbar***), in the middle a ***Raid or Commune***, and at the apex, a ***Hima*** (***elaka***). At the village level democracy is direct; it is based on adult male francise. Each village has its own General Assembly and an Executive Council with well defined powers and functions. At the ***Raid*** and ***Hima*** levels, democracy is indirect and representative. At the village level an individual is a unit, at the ***Raid*** level, a clan is a unit, whereas at the ***Hima*** levels both a clan and a village are a unit. Each ***Raid*** has its own General Assembly consisting of all adult male members of the ***Raid,*** and a ***Raid*** Council which consists of representatives elected by the major clans of the area under its jurisdiction and which perform administrative, executive and judicial functions. At the ***Hima*** level we find two institutions, one is the ***Syiem*** in Council which consists of the ***Syiem*** and all the members of the ***Raid*** Council within the ***Hima*** which is the highest administrative, executive and judicial body. The other is the general assembly of the Hima or ***Darbar Hima,*** which consists of all the members of the ***Syiem***-in-Council and the representatives elected by the people of the villages within the ***Hima.*** This ***Darbar*** formulates all policy matters and makes final decisions on all matters referred to it by the ***Syiem***-in-Council. David Roy gives the details of the administration of the country, there are three classes of people: (1) the ***Syiems, Lyngdoh, Wahadadars*** and ***Sirdars;*** (2) the ***Lyngskors, Myntries, Basans*** (rulers of ***raids***), ***Dollois;*** and (3) the ***Raid.*** The ***Lyngkors*** (they preside over the council meetings) and the ***Mynries*** are the ***Bakhraws*** (***nobility*** / elders). They are the people who belong to the powerful clans. Along with them the ***Basans*** and ***Dollois*** who elect a ***Syiem***. The ***Bakhraws*** together with the ***Syiem*** and ***Lyngdoh*** form the ***Darbar*** of the ***Hima*** (Roy, 1994:116 117).

In Khasi states, the administrative arrangement were however, not as elaborate as those of the Jaintia Kingdom. But it is noticed that there is a three-tier arrangement in all the states. The ***Syiems*** in the Khasi states are assisted by a number of ***Myntries*** in the state administration. The state has also several divisions described by Gordon as ***raj*** and by Bareh as ***communes,*** locally known as ***raid***. Besides ***Myntries,*** there are the ***Lyngdohs,*** the ***Basans*** and the ***Lyngskors*** who act as the ***Syiem***'s deputy governors. The ***Rangbah Shnongs*** (Village headman) who are also called ***Sirdars, Matabors Majis,*** etc. function at the grass root level. It is therefore noted that the Khasi States with three-tier administrative arrangements are essentially different from other forms of tribal polity, which are nothing more than a village polity (Bareh, 1964:37–38; Gordon, 1907:66–75). Hence, the kingdom was therefore so structured as to suit the needs of a stratified society. This stratification, however, was not as rigid as exist in class-based societies. Even then it was such as to suggest the existence of landed gentry who would naturally wield political power. There are also reasons to believe that this landed gentry would use the customary land tenure in a fashion, which would help perpetuate their rule. Gassah has aptly described this situation (Gassah, 1980). According to him traditional pattern of authority, leadership structure and administration was vested in persons belonging to certain original clan or clans (***Kurs***) and other clans were deprived of this privilege. This pattern was followed in all the three tiers of administration in the pre-British era and even after that period (*Ibid.,* 100).

Shri Christobin Rymbai of Jowai, who relates the system with five Kpohs (Wombs) further, supports the above statement—

i. ***Shri Kpoh***
ii. ***Lai koph***
iii. ***Ar Kpoh***
iv. Saw Kpoh
v. San Kpoh

From these *Kpohs* came a number of *Kurs*(class), these five ***Kpohs*** would provide different officials, both religious and secular.

II and III Kpoh could appoint ***Dollois.*** From ***V Kpoh and I*** the ***Pattors*** came. They appoint ***Lyngdoh clan of Saw Kpoh*** as functionaries in the ***darbar. Dollois*** and the ***Basans*** also came from the ***Saw Kpoh.***

Sri Kynpham Singh gives other picture about the Khasi States administrative arrangements. "The ***raids*** took the form of small oligarchies, which federated to emerge as states with the clans of the ***Lyngdohs, Basans, or Bakhraws,*** as the founding members, sitting at the helm of the affairs through their respective clan representatives". He also feels that the ***Syiems*** of the Khasi States did not have much real power and the ruling clans such as the `***Khadar Kurs'*** (12 clans) of Cherra were at the helm of affairs and Cherra ***Syiemship*** in the prototype of all the ***Syiemships*** in the hills (Kynpham, 1985:1–8). Our study reflects that in Cherra, the ***Mantries*** of the twelve ruling clans can nominate a ***Syiem,*** and forty-eight ***Kurs*** elect 12 ***Mantries*** who assume the responsibility only when the original twelve fail to reach an unanimous decision. If a heir is disqualified from succeeding to the ***Syiemship,*** the next in the order of succession must be appointed as the ***Syiem.*** For expository convenience the following case studies were undertaken:

Case Study I:

The ***Syiemship*** of Sohra is situated in Cherrapunji sub–division of East Khasi Hills district of Meghalaya. This ***Syiemship's elaka (Hima)*** covers more than 112 villages out of which 93 are recognised and the rest are yet to be recognised formally by the Government. 12 Clans including 6 executive members representing from their ***raids*** regard the ***Darbar*** of the ***Syiem*** as Executive ***Darbar,*** which comprises 12 elected

Mantris. Under this ***Syiemship,*** it is to be noted that the ***Syiem*** cannot be a Christian. Under this ***Syiemship*** the following three-tier structure is maintained:

	Institution	*Head of the Institution (hiefs)*
1.	Hima	Syiem
2.	Raid Darbar	Sirdar
3.	Village Darbar	Village Headman (***Rangbah Shnong***)

In this Syiemship the Village Darbar being at the grass-root level gets more importance. It is a non-political elected body. Even the mode of election was quite democratic. The ***Mantris*** were elected directly by their respective clans. They enjoy life long tenure. The executive body member enjoys only 5 years' tenurship like a MLA. The elected ***Syiem*** requires written confirmation from the KHADC to hold his position. In this regard Chief Executive Member (CEM) of ADC gets it pass through the Executive Committee of ADC, and finally the sanad confirm the position of ***Syiem*** as well as ***Mantries.***

Case Study II: Khyrim Syiemship:

Almost all affairs of the tribe are settled at the ***raid*** level. Traditionally, the officials of the ***raid Darbar*** are from the noble and royal clans, which continue to be governed by the same tradition. See table-1.

Nongkrem, Nonglori, Mawlieh, Mawshai, Nongkynrieh and Lawai are full-fledged raids. Mawshai, Laishaiat, Thyuroit, Jongksha, Mawblang, Sarikari, Lapngar, Hynmiew Shnong, Pra Blang, Khadar Bang, Langshi Kleih, Saw raid and Rishnong Siem are ***sub-raids*** or sub-units. The ***Darbar Raids*** of Nongkrem and Nongbri have joint jurisdiction over the ***sub raids*** of Sarikari (comprising 10 sub-raids) lapngar, Hynmiew Shnong and Pra Blang (8 ***sub-raids***). Similarly the Darbar raid of Mawlieh has control over the *sub-raids* of Langshi Klieh. ***Saw-raids*** (4 ***raids***) and Ri Shnong Siem are directly under the ***Syiem*** of Khyrim. Besides, the sub-raids of Nongseh and Nongumlong of Mylliem State are under the jurisdiction of the Khyrim Syiemship for all religious purposes.

Every *raid* has one ***Lyngdoh*** and four ***Myntries*** whereas the ***Raid*** Nongkrem has one ***Lynskor*** besides one ***Lyngdoh*** and four ***Myntries. Lynskor*** is considered as the Prime Minister of the ***Syiemship***. Hence, for the entire ***hima*** there is one ***Lynskor***. He hails from ***Mylliem-Ngap clan***. His own male clan members elect him. He presides over the ***Syiem Darbar*** in the absence of the ***Syiem***. His election is generally conducted in the presence of six ***Lyngdohs*** from six raids and the ***Syiem***. His term of office is for life. The ***Syiem Darbar*** has the power to remove the ***Lynskor***, if the latter is found inefficient or guilty of contravening the traditional norms.

The ***Lyngdoh*** exercises both secular and religious powers. He is elected only from the ***Lyngdoh*** (priest) clan. He enjoys certain special privileges and rights in his ***raid***. The *Lyngdoh* of Nongkrem claims superior social, ritual and political status compared with his counterparts, such as those of Nonglori, Mawlieh, Nongkynrih and \lawai, for he is the priest of ***Syiem's*** family and has to assist and advise the ***Syiem*** in all religious and ritualistic matters. The ***Lyngdoh*** in his own ***raid*** presides over the ***Darbar raid*** and important religious ceremonies.

Each of the raids has four ***Myntries*** (ministers) who come from the royal clan. The *Myntries* are the advisors to the ***Syiem*** at the state level. At the ***raid*** level ***Myntries*** and ***Lyngdohs*** are *the* ***Bakhraws*** (noblemen) who constitute the ***Darbar raid***. They are the elected representatives of the male members of their respective clans. There are 24 elected ***Myntries*** and three ***Syiem*** nominated ***Myntries*** for the whole of ***Khyrim Syiemship***. The ***Myntries*** have two duties: (1) to function as co-rulers with the *Syiem;* (2) to elect the *Syiem.* The *Syiem's Darbar* is an executive, administrative and judicial body. It consists of the *Syiem*, one *Lynskor, Six Lyngdohs* and twenty-seven *Myntries.*

The ***sub-raids*** are under the charge of ***Basans*** or ***Sirdars.*** The superintendents of village markets are also called ***Basans. Basans and Sirdars*** are under the jurisdiction of the ***Lyngdohs*** and ***Myntries*** of the ***raid.*** The ***Darbar raid*** has the general supervision of the officials of the ***sub-raids.*** But the ***Basans*** have almost similar functions as those of the ***Bakhraws.***

The ***Bakhraws*** are the elders like the ***Lynskors, Lyngdohs*** and ***Myntries.*** Only the male members of a group of villages elect the ***Sirdars*** and ***Basans.***

Case Study III:

Mylliem is the prime ***Hima*** under East Khasi Hills District of Meghalaya. This Syiemship ***elaka (Hima)*** covers 345 villages with a population of 486085 out of which 358341 are tribals. This ***Hima*** also covers some villages under the Ribhoi District. It was a misfortune for the Khasi Hills that a great heroic leader, Bormanik ***Syiem*** of Shillong was trapped by the British troops in May 1830, which forced him to surrender. Contemporary accounts say that **Bormanik** fled to Bhutan or Tibet where he began to negotiate for military assistance, but never returned to his home state. In the meantime, there arose mutual disagreement among the electors of the Shillong State because the ***'Bakhraws'*** (Elders) of the ***raid*** Mylliem refused to accept **Singmanik** as their ***Syiem.*** Civil war ensued within the state that culminated in the bifurcation of Shillong State into Khyrim and Mylliem states(Lyngdoh, op.cit).

In Mylliem, there is an Electoral College consisting of five ***Mantries,*** two ***Basans,*** one ***Lyngdoh*** and the rest are the headmen known as ***Matabors.*** The total number of electors is twenty-five. But the United Khasi and Jaintia Hills Autonomous District Act, 1957 provides for inclusion of the

Table -1
KHYRIM SYIEMSHIP

Raids	*Officials*			*Sub-Raids*	*Officials*
	Tribes	*Nos.*	*Clans*		
Nongkrem	Lynskor	1	Mylliem Ngap	Mawsjao	Basan
				Laosjmat	
				Thynrolt	
				Jongksha	
	Lyngdoh	1			
	Myntries	3	Pyngrup		
			Mylliem Pdah		
			Warbah		
			Khyriem Mujat		
Nongbri	Lyngdoh	1	Lyngdoh Nongbri	Maw Blang	Basan
	Myntries	2	Swar		
			Synnah		
			Mawthou		
			Kharummuid		
Mawlieh	Lyngdoh	1	Lyngdoh Mawlieh	Maw Blang	Basan
	Myntries	2	Khongsngi		
			Khongsti		
			Khongwir		
			Nongrum		

contd...

contd...

Raids	*Officials*			*Sub-Raids*	*Officials*
	Tribes	*Nos.*	*Clans*		
Mawshai	Lyngdoh Myntries	1 2	Lyngdoh Mawshai Mongspung Mawthoh Ryntong Muwa	Sarikrai (10 sub-raids) Iapngar Hynniew Shnong Pira Blang (8 sub-raids)	Basan
Lawai	Lyngdoh Myntries	1 2	Lyngdoh Lawai Sohtun Lawai Sawkhr Kharsati Synteng	—	—
Nongkynrih	Lyngdoh Myntries	1 2	Lyngdoh Nongkynrih Mylliem Nongrum Rynjah Nongkynrih	Langshi Khlieh Nongiri Massar Mukhim Rasangbad Rymphlang Mukertilla	**Sirdar**

Source: Information collected from the concerned Local Government.

representatives of the twenty-three clans of "***Raid San Shnong***" in the Electoral College. The present total strength of the Electoral College is forty-eight. A simple majority may elect the ***Syiem*** of Mylliem. As in the Khyrim State, the electors, for sufficient reasons, may disqualify the heir.

There are 9 constituencies under the ***Mylleim Syiem's*** jurisdiction, which encompasses about 1000 villages of the East Khasi Hills District and the Ri–Bhoi District. These areas are much rich and a maximum no. of wet lands are there mainly for paddy broom, ginger, potatoes, turmeric, chillis, rubber and tea (newly introduced) cultivation.

The Syiem institution is not formally linked with the ADC; it is rather forced link. The ***Darbar of Syiem*** is not a statutory one; rather it is a traditional organisation of the Khasis, where every citizen under this institution feels completely secure. According to the ***Syiem*** their institution is three tiers and it is formed through direct and indirect election. In the villages the villagers elect their headman and members through direct election. In the ***Syiem Darbar*** the elected members who are the representatives of the people elect the ***Syiem***. In the village level the headman conducts the ***Darbar*** elections.

There is no tenure fixed for the ***Darbar*** of the ***Syiem***. In all the bodies, the tenure of the headman (the ***Sardar***) or the ***Syiem*** depends on the proficiency and efficiency of the elected leader in serving his people. He takes the responsibilities of his office with utmost sincerity. But the elected persons are from the specific clans, which indicates that the position is open, for example, the ***Syiem Clan*** in the case of ***Syiemship*** and ***Lyngdoh Clan*** for ***Lyngdohship*** and so on.

The Duties of Syiem towards his People:

The first and foremost duty of the *Syiem* towards his people is that of a guardian or as a parent. This traditional value is embodied in the ***Syiems***. The ***Syiem*** acts like a ***Paiem*** ('Pa' means mother and father combined into one single parent and '***aiem***' means 'the loving one'). Hence the first duty of the ***Syiem*** is that of loving parents. The ***Syiem*** has to look after his people not as subjects but as children. All things be it a matter of importance or conflicts are solved through discussions; for that matter the time is not a constraint, but people should satisfied with the judgment. In cases where matters cannot be solved through discussions, the ***Syiem*** takes on the judicial mantle, and with a strong hand decides cases in accordance with customs, traditions and age old laws of the people.

There is social control within the villages. Only when the law and order situation in the villages goes out of hand (as in the case of 1996 incident) the matter reaches the ***syiem***. The Khasi society does not believe in imposing things on its people. People are tradition bound and rarely do they dare to defy the law and order situation. The ADC, according to the *syiem*, has been trying to create instability in the ***Syiemship*** that is beneficial in the electoral system of the District Council. The ***Darbar Syiem***, which is a partyless democracy, is very much opposed to this.

The sources of income are the resources owned by the ***Darbar***. Major sources are the markets (royalty or toll is collected from these markets). The minor sources of income are the mineral resources and forests.

The ***Syiem's*** opinion about the District Council is not very good. According to him it is of no use for the people. It exists only in namesake but actually it does not look after the people, it is the question of whether to protecting them or cooperating with them for any purpose. Even it does not involve the people and take them into confidence for any work even if the matter is related to the people. Hence, it makes no difference for the ***Syiem*** whether it exists or not, but the three-tier ***Darbar Syiem*** will do its best for the welfare of the people.

Darbar Owned different types of Forest are:

i. Clan Forests ii. Individual Forests iii. Community Forests iv. Sacred Forests vii.Village Forests viii. ***Raid*** Forests ix. ***Hima*** Forests.

Case Study IV:

Hima Nongstoin is located in the West Khasi Hills district of Meghalaya, which is also one among the largest Khasi states covering 278 villages with a population of 56794 out of which 55326 are tribals, spreading over 3 blocks.

In this ***Hima,*** there is a large electoral ***Darbar*** consisting of sixty members, two ***Mantries,*** forty-one ***Lyngdohs,*** twenty-five ***Sirdars,*** one ***Lyngskor,*** and one ***Basan.*** The ***Lyngdohs*** are the heads of the priestly clans. The ***Syiem*** chooses the ***Sirdars*** and ***Lyngskor*** who are the agents of the ***Syiem*** for the collection of revenue. The ***Syiem,*** with the approval of the male adults of the village, appoints them. A simple majority in the electoral ***Darbar*** is sufficient for the election of a ***Syiem***. If an heir is disqualified, the ***Darbar*** is bound to nominate the next in the successions, and if he is also disqualified, the next in the order of succession should be elected.

Case Study V:
Hima Shella Wahadadarship

The title of the Chief of Shella, is undoubtedly not a traditional Khasi Chief's designation. Etymologically, the term ***'Wahadadar'*** has a Persian origin. It is derived from the persian word, ***Oh'da' dar or' uhdo-dar*** (Gordon, 1914:75), as Gurdon puts it, which means high officials. The ***Wahadadars*** were however, lower ranking village civil and revenue officials, though the literal meaning of their designation may mean otherwise.

In the Shella confederacy formerly there were four *Wahadadars*. The people elected these Chiefs for a period of three years each. At present only one *Wahadadar* is elected from the whole confederacy on the basis of adult suffrage for five years. But the candidate must be a native of Shella.

In this *Hima*, there are 36 villages covering two blocks with a population of 11159 of which 9299 are the tribals. A nominal head called *Wahadadar* heads this *Hima*. Under this *Hima* there are villages with their own headman and a *Darbar*. It is a federation of villages. Each *Darbar* consists of 8-10 members and one secretary. The ADC, through sanad, also confirms their positions. Their tenure including *Wahadadar* is only for five years. Unlike *Syiem* and *Dolloi*, the *Wahadadar* including his functionaries may be chosen irrespective of their caste, creed and clans.

Functions of Wahadadars under Mughals and Raja of Jaintia:

They were appointed as the highest officials in the villages who were assisted by the Choudhurys (revenue collectors) in the collection of tolls and revenues, in the adjudiciation of petty disputes and similar other duties such as the maintenance of peace or police duties.

Functions of Wahadadars under The British Rule:

Under the British rule Wahadadars administered justice, each of the four members of the council excersing only one vote, collected tolls and duties, leased out lime quarries and orange grooves for royalty and maintained peace in the state.

Case Study VI:
Hima Sohing (Lyngdoh)

It mainly falls under the West Khasi Hills district of Meghalaya, but some of the villages fall under Ri-bhoi and East Khasi Hills district also. There are all together 83 villages, which covers four C.D. blocks. Total population is 21302 of which 2341 are tribals.

Under this *Hima* there are four *Lyngdoh raids* (four sub-unit of the *elaka*), which form the Electoral College to elect the *Lyngdoh*. Election is unanimous. But if the elected *Lyngdoh* is not accepted by the people, the male adults hold the popular election and elect the *Lyngdoh*.. These *Lyngdoh raids* after electing their *Lyngdoh* form the executive *Darbar* for administration of the entire *elaka,* along with five *Myntries*. These *Myntries* are from five clans. *Lyngdoh* is also an administrative head. The executive *Darbar* also appoints a Secretary to assist the executive *Darbar*. The entire *Lyngdoh raids* have got their own respective *Darbar* and separate village court under their respective jurisdiction.

Case Study VII:
Nongpoh Hima Sirdarship

This *Sirdarship* falls under the Ri-bhoi district covering one block with 74 villages. The total population of this *elaka* is 20157, of which 17383 are tribals, the rest are non-tribals.

A Sirdar with 3 Myntris and 7 Lyngdoh who are the priests heads the executive Darbar of this Sirdarship. The position of *Sirdar* is hereditary through clan. *Myntris* are also hereditary through clan. The villages under this *elaka* have their own *Darbar* comprising 7-9 members with a Secretary and a Chairman.

SET-UP OF NON-KHASI STATES

During the British administration in the Khasi and the Jaintia Hills, the United Khasi and Jaintia Hills District was divided into two Sub-Divisions: Shllong and Jowai. Shillong became the District Head Quarters of the Deputy Commissioner and Jowai was placed under the charge of a European Subordinate Magistrate. The Jaintia Hills, Shillong and 34 villages in the Khasi Hills were declared British territory. The rest of the Khasi Hills included in the Twenty Five native Khasi states, which had treaties with the British, was declared as within the District but outside British India for which the Deputy Commissioner functioned as Political Agent of the government. By the Sixth Schedule to the Constitution of India all territories are now merged into the Autonomous District Council areas except the three wards of Shillong Municipality viz. Cantonment, Jail Road and the European ward, which are now known as normal areas of administration.

The British territories in the Khasi Hills were placed in-charge of a titular heads called ***Sirdars,*** and the whole of the Jaintia Hills under ***Dollois*** whose number was raised to nineteen by splitting large territories to create new units(Rymbai, 1998).

Dollois **of Jaintia Hills:**

The elaka of ***Dolloi*** in the Jaintia Hills was part of the Jaintia Kingdom. It was however the only Khasi states which were made into a British area. It was on March 15, 1835, that Captain Lister, delivered in the court of the Syiem of Jaintia, Rajendra Singh, the decree of the Governor General of India from Fort William, Calcutta, that the British had taken possession of the Jaintia Paraghanas of Jaintiapur. The citizen of ***Hima*** Jaintia however resisted this move and attacked the camp of Captain Lister at Amwi on August 22, 1835. Syiem Rajendra Singh of ***Hima*** Jaintia had, however, without consultation of the ***Dolloi*** and the clan (***Kur***) of the ruling lineage, ceded the hill position of ***Hima*** Jaintia to the British and accepted a pension of Rs.500 per month. In 1951, the Assam Govt. had transferred the Jaintia sub-division areas of Block I and II including Lambang – Nongphyllent to the Mikir hills district of Assam, now known as the Karbi Anglong district, which came into existence on November17, 1951.

Traditionally, in Khasi states there used to be thirty states, each under a titular head called ***Syiem***, twenty-nine of which were in the Khasi hills and one in the Jaintia hills. But in the Jaintia hills originally there were twelve ***Dollois***, independent of each other, but later they chose one ***Syiem*** to be their titular head. After their occupation of the land, the British annexed seven states in their territories. They also demoted the status of eight states; three of them were placed under lesser heads called ***Lyngdohs***, five under still lesser heads called ***Sirdars***, and fifteen remained under ***Syiems***. The so-called British territories - thirty-one villages in Khasi hills and the whole of Jaintia hills, comprised not only the six abolished states but also villages taken from the remaining fifteen sates on one plea or the other. The British territories in the Khasi Hills were placed incharge of titular heads called ***Sirdars*** and the whole of the Jaintia Hills under Dollois whose number was raised to nineteen by splitting larger territories to create new units.

In the Jaintia hills district unlike the Khasi hills, there are 20 ***Dollois*** and one ***Sirdarship***, out of which 12 were of ministerial rank during the British period.

As far as the Jaintia Hills are concerned, the picture is quite different. After the annexation of the Jaintia hills in 1835, it is not clear how the British Government pushed the so important functionaries like the ***Lyngskor, Lyngdohs and Myntris*** into the background and brought the position of ***Dollois*** into prominence.

As per the statement of A.J,Moffat Mills in 1853 the ***Dollois*** were the officers of the British Government, They had a certain number of Projects or villages under their charge and they investigated all petty cases of a civil and criminal nature within their district. The British probably wanted to administer the area through the ***Dollois*** and hence retained them as area Chief at the discretion of the community on condition that every 3 years they had to be re-elected by the people. Till the new ***Dolloi*** was elected the position of the out going ***Dolloi*** was retained.

Each ***Dolloiship*** is administered by the ***Dolloi*** assisted by officials called ***Pattors*** and ***Sangot,*** each having his own specified responsibilities. In the past the ***Dollois*** were more than temporal heads–they exercised executive, political and magisterial powers but they also had religious duties to perform. Although, they were not paid any salaries, they were provided with service land for their maintenance. They apparently paid nominal tribute to the King, usually assessed at one goat for each village. This token tribute continued to be accepted by the British in the early years of their administration.

Next to ***Dolloi*** is the Pator. He looks after the administration of the ***Dolloiship*** in case of any vacancy due to the death, removal or incapacity of the ***Dolloi,*** and remains in office until a new ***Dolloi*** is elected. At the lowest rung is the village Elder or Headman who is usually elected by the ***Darbar*** of male adults. The village elders preside over the session of the village council, ordinarily composed of all the male adults of the village, with the elder people as the advisors.

The above are the administrative units recognised by usage and all of them have continued in existence till the present.

In our study we covered two ***Dollois,*** namely, ***Nartiang*** and ***Nongbah,*** The ***Nartiang*** covers 52 villages under the jurisdiction of only one C.D. Block. The population under this Dolloi is 16984 of which 1678 are tribals. The Nongbah covers 10 villages in two CD blocks with a population of 9969, all of which are the tribals.

Set up of Jaintia Hills District Council:

In 1952 the Six Schedules to the Constitution provided for the creation of District Council in the Autonomous Districts of Assam, which came to be known as United Khasi and Jaintia Hills District Council. Six members in the 24-member council represented the Jaintia Hills. In 1957 a section of the public began to press their case for the establishment of a separate District Council for the Jaintia Hills for administrative convenience. On the recommendation of the Commission set up to enquire into the matter, the Govt. of Asssam in 1964 issued a notification announcing the creation of a separate District Council. This council was called the Jaintia Hills Autonomous District Council. The first election following the issue of this notification took place in 1967 and the first constitutionally elected District Council then took over the administration of the District.

The number of members in the JHADC (both elected and nominated) upto the 1978 elections was 18. List of past and present electoral constituencies are given in Appendix.

The role assigned to the District Council by the Constitution is to safeguard the interests of the tribal people in respect of their lands, their social customs and practices and their culture, and to foster primary education within the District. It is also empowered to pass laws relating to the above objectives and regarding levies of revenue, tolls etc. to meet the cost of the administration.

5

Village Council: An Institution of Grassroot Level Administration in Meghalaya

The main features of traditional tribal administration in Meghalaya are the democratic content from the grass-root level to the top echelons of the administration. In the Khasi and the Jaintia hills the village is the basic unit of administration. Families of the same clans living together in a particular location or areas for cultivation and other purposes generally form villages in these hills.

Every Khasi village has its own local tribal assembly called Village ***Darbar or Darbar Shnong***. All the adult male inhabitants of the village are required to attend the sessions of the ***Darbar***. The meetings are presided over by ***Rangbah Shnong*** (Village Headman). He functions for the welfare of the village. The village sanitation, water supply, health, roads, and schools are under the jurisdiction of the ***Darbar***. The ***Darbar*** is also responsible for protecting and strengthening the morale of the community. Petty quarrels and the village headman in consultation with village elders (***Bakhraws***) amicably settles disputes.

The administration of justice in the Khasi society is another important function of the Khasi ***Darbar*** where punishment for crime may be either reformatory or punitive in character. The first type is called ***Pynsuk*** and the second is known as

Saja. Reformatory punishment is carried out in the form of imprisonment for a specific period or by the payment of a fine to be paid either in cash or in kind. This is precisely in the case of theft, cheating, or acts intended to inflict physical injury on any person. Capital punishment is awarded for murder or castings of a magic spell on any one so as to make a victim lose his normal senses. In the case of capital punishment accused is beaten with clubs to death. The method is called by the ***Khasi u tangon u lymban***. Hurling him down a precipice was also practiced.

There are also other types of punishment known as ***jylla kharit and pyndair diengsong***. This practice involves sending a convicted person into exile. Such persons have to have their heads shaven in three patches, at the very sight of which people at once know that he is an outcast. Such persons have no more any rights and obligations in the family, and are denied the right of residence in any locality. The practice **of** ***pandit diengsong*** involves the confinement of a criminal in a cell with his hands and feet tied to wooden poles.

Capital punishment resulting in the death of a criminal is generally carried out outside a locality to ward off evil spirits called ***ka tynet ka smer*** by the Khasis. If this is not done, the belief is that such spirits may cause depredation to the people of a locality.

Punishment awarded in respect of other civil cases of mild character involves payment of either cash or giving pigs or both, according to the nature of the case. The practice of giving pigs to the ***Syiem's Darbar*** is done with a view to serving a warning to the accused that he should not indulge in a habit of opposing conciliatory measure offered while in the process of hearing of a case. A fine amounting to Rs. 550/- is imposed in the case of cohabiting with a man or woman from his or her own clan. The practice of giving an opportunity to the accused party on his prayer for reduction of the fine is also recorded.

According to Khasi practice, justice is very much a part of custom. They are inviolable and through out the ages, they have proved their rigidity. No attempts at modifying the practice relating to the administration of justice in the Khasi Hills have been recorded.

Following the traditional practice prevalent among the Khasis, the United Khasi – Jaintia Hills, Autonomous (Administration of Justice) Rules, 1953 have also adopted the same principles. The rules have given to the village courts or ***Raj (raid)*** courts the powers to try civil cases and criminal cases of mild character. Cases involving punishment in accordance with the IPC are, however, outside their jurisdiction. Such lower courts also have the power to impose a fine amounting to not more than Rs.25/- on persons absconding from the judgement of the courts. Absconding is known to ***the Khasis as Ka bein dorbar***. It is regarded as abstention with a view to denying the authority of the court, and any repetition of such act may even lead to eviction of a person from the locality in which he resides.

The Khasi concept of law is basically abstract in as much as they do not have written laws. The basic foundation of law is custom and for that reason, laws are regarded as rigid and inviolable. The Khasis also believe that the law must be related to morality. It is only when that condition is fulfilled that justice finds its impartial application. We may therefore, consider a Khasi as a socialist in the sense that he recognises that all persons are equal before law. Decisions of courts are regarded ultra virus if they do not conform to accepted customary usage. Because of the importance attached to custom, the Khasis have also developed and practised the principle of give and take in any dispute; if conciliation fails, the case is referred to the court. Fighting a case or ***mokotduma*** is considered a social taboo in Khasi society, which should be avoided.

The village headman thus handles and enforces law and order. He discharges the dual functions of a magistrate and police officers in the administration of the village. His verdicts are almost always unequivocal and imperative on the village community. The village courts are the statutory body constituted by the District Council with a Chairman and Vice-Chairman. The members of the District Council cannot be chairman or vice-chairman of the village courts. The chairman of the village courts is ***Dolloi, Sirdar, Syiem-Raid, Basan, Lyngdoh, Lyngskor*** or Headman. The vice-chairman shall be one of the members of the village court. Another member is its Secretary. Complicated cases are referred to the chief of the state, or the head of the commune (***Sirdar***). The headman is expected to inspire and influence the village community by his personality. In the absence of the village priest (***Lyngdoh***), the headman also officiates as the priest when prayers are offered to the ancestral deities. He presides over the village ceremonies connected with divination. It is his duty to see to the payment of tributes to the chief or the territorial headman by the village community. Their ***Rangbah Shnong*** accompanies villagers when they go to file important cases at such appellate courts as the commune courts(***Raid Darbar***), the ***Syiem Darbar*** or now-a-days the court of the District Councils.

He transmits and relays the messages and orders of his political superior, including those of the Chief of the State, to his village people. In the present administrative set up both the Government and District Council attaches a good deal of value to the function and services of the village headman. In spite of the onerous duty discharged by him, however, the prerogatives of the village headman are not unlimited. If the village is a political unit, the smallest unit in the Khasi hierarchy is the ***Darbar Kur*** (the clan council). This unit may be described as the plinth, which embodies in itself the consciousness of village unity and a manifestation of the interdependence. Among the members linking it to a central authority. Its influence rises in the ascending scale in successive higher tiers that are built over it. In order to see the functioning of *Darbar* we carried out four case studies in four districts mentioned below:

Case Study I:
Shella Village Headman under East Khasi Hills District:

Shella village *Darbar* consists of 26 members who select one Secretary for the *Darbar* to execute the function. They even sit for two to three times in a month if necessary. At least 1/3 members are required to be present during the time of meeting in the *Darbar* to form the quorum. If 9 members do not attend, they adjourn the *Darbar* on that particular day. The District Council, through *Sanad,* finally confirms the Headman who is elected by the people of the village. He and his functionaries all give voluntary services for the welfare of the people of Shella village.

Shella Village Court:

In Shella Village Court generally discussions on judicial matters are held and the headman of the village is the chairman of the village court. This court consists of 3-6 members, out of which one is selected as the vice-chairman, who is to function in the absence of the chairman. The term of the court and the chairman is 5 years. The same headman continues for another term if none contests for the post. This is again subject to the condition of his acceptance. Generally after 10 years term they conduct fresh election. The other members however follow the usual procedure. The District Council, through *Sanad,* also confirms the position of the members.

A woman cannot be a member of *Darbar,* which is due to customary law. They cannot even participate in any activities of *Darbar.*

Regarding selection of development activities either funded by the state government or MDC's projects, the *Darbar* takes decisions. Even prioritising the projects/any issues is left to the ***Darbar.*** Once the decision is taken, every member extends full participation and makes the project great success.

Sources of Funds:

They do not get direct fund from the central and the state government. But they get fund from MLAs and MDCs for select works like footpath making, repairing of ***bazar*** sheds etc.

In order to strengthen the ***Darbar,*** the public from the village gives contributions; the amount of contribution is however not fixed. At times, the District Council obliges them with some fund for specific purposes. Their involvement in the government work is only for the selection of beneficiaries. They are not directly linked with District Council. In fact their requirements are discussed first at the village ***Darbar,*** then placed to *Wahadadar,* and then it is sent to the District Council for approval. However, they some times feel it is a lengthy process, but they do not have the right to approach the District Council directly. Since they have cordial relation with their ***elaka*** head (i.e., the ***Wahadadar***), they generally do not face much difficulty.

Sometimes it so happens that they cannot reach decisions in the village court. In such a circumstance they refer the case to their ***elaka*** court (i.e., ***Wahadadar Darbar***) for further decision. Generally they solve the matters/ cases related to land disputes/marriage or divorce etc. through their customary law. But regarding crime they generally report to the police.

The ***Darbar*** takes democratic decisions through public opinion. If the people reject a decision taken by the Darbar on a certain cases it is generally referred to ***Wahadadar.*** At present it seems the ***Darbar*** functionaries are quite happy with the functioning of their ***Darbar*** and system. However, they feel financial constraints, as for which, they think, can be overcome by donations and government support.

Case Study II :
(New Nongstoin Village Darbar) West Khasi Hills District:

The people of the village select the village headman. The village headman is locally known as ***Sardar***. After the selection the ***Syiem*** of Nongstoin appoints him. According to the ***Sardar, Darbar*** is essential for the purpose of village administration as well as for the welfare and development of the village and its people. But interestingly he does not see any difference in the functioning of their ***Darbar*** during the previous time and after Meghalaya got the statehood. This indicates that the ***Darbar*** is perhaps not very liable to change which comes in the way of taking up development programmes. Its executive body consists of 13 members. There are some conditions observed as to the eligibility of the membership:

i. He should be a permanent resident of the village at least for five years continuously.

ii. He must be from the same village.

iii. He should be good natured (preferably educated) and well disciplined.

iv. A good record of regular attendance at all the *Darbar* meetings.

v. Women are not allowed in the *Darbar*.

The reasons for not involving women in the ***Darbar*** is as follows:

In Khasi society the women are highly respected. Since the ***Darbar*** deals with political matters, so they do not prefer or support the women participation in political affairs of the ***Darbar.***

The ***Darbar*** conducts two types of meetings:

(i) **General meeting:** (***Darbar Shnong***) This is rather a public meeting of the village. Those who are 18 years of age and above can attend this meeting. But students' presence is not compulsory. This meeting is held generally once in a year. But, if necessary, it may held many be held many times within 2-3 months. No one is fined even if he is absent.

(ii) **Executive body meeting** (***Jingialong Ki rangbah Shnong***): The members of this executive body meeting are selected in general meeting. There are 12 members in this body excluding the ***Sardar***. They are required to sort out important matters. They even meet twice/thrice in a month.

A member failing to attend the meeting as scheduled has to reply to the **Sardar** for not attending the meeting giving proper reason. If the reason is justified, he is neither subjected to any punishment nor has he to pay fine. But if this becomes a regular practice, then he is expelled from the ***Darbar*** with a notice approved by all other members.

He agrees that things like policy formulations, priority fixing, selection of areas for development and distribution of government grants should be either entrusted to the village ***Darbar*** or to the ***Syiem***'s Court, rather than to the District Councils.

Sources of Funds :

i. Contributions/donations as per the capability of the villagers.

ii. Funds are also available from MDCs, MPs and MLAs, but very negligible amount. In fact they have receive only Rs.10,000/- during the last 18 years. This amount was given to the ***Syiem*** for purchasing a football ground, but the actual amount invested for the purpose was Rs.1,00,000/-

Involvement with Government /District Council :

They are involved only in formulation and implementation of government projects, such as road construction, footbridge etc.

They do not have any link with the District Council; their link is only with the ***Syiem***. Village ***Darbar*** generally confine themselves to their own affairs like land dispute of the village, minor crime and punishment; and development issues like education, sanitation, road construction etc. Only the disputed cases unsolved at the village ***Darbar***'s level are referred to ***Hima Darbar***, i.e. ***Syiem***'s court.

Powers and Functions :

The village ***Darbar*** enjoys the following powers and functions accordingly:

Judicial – crime and punishment

Administrative – maintaining law and order, peace and harmony in the village.

But the ***Sardar*** has opined that there need to be changes regarding the powers as follows:

1. More judicial power is required, as these days he has to frequently refer cases to the *Hima Darbar*.
2. More powers are required for overall functioning of the system.
3. Since he cannot realise any tax from any body, so his financial strength is very much limited, which needs to be enhanced.

As regards financial matters he feels that he should be allowed to share tax with the ***Syiem*** as well as the District Council. He even feels that the government tax should be shared with his ***Darbar***.

***Case Study III* : *Nongpo Headman* under Ri-bhoi District**

The Nongpo headman is a ***Lyngdoh,*** who feels that the village ***Darbar*** is essential for the welfare of the people of the village. However, he feels that the status of his ***Syiem*** was reduced during the British period, otherwise he would have been working under a ***Syiem***. However, they feel no difference so far as their function is concerned.

They hold ***Darbar*** for general, judicial as well as other matters. For general matters they held ***Darbar*** once in a year, but for judicial matters they hold several ***Darbars,*** if necessary, two-three ***Darbars*** in a year to dispose of the cases. Critical cases are referred to ***Sardar Hima;*** i.e. court of the ***elaka*** chief. There are total 7-8 members in a village ***Darbar***; they come from different clans. The headman feels that ***Darbar*** is essential for prioritizing the development activities, like drinking water, construction of footpath etc.;as also for keeping record of birth and death.

To become a ***Darbar*** member the following qualities are required:

i. A well disciplined personality.

ii. A fairly intelligent person who may command respect.

The headman feels that it is difficult to reply why women cannot be a member of Darbar. But since it is a tradition, they simply respect the tradition. But women are allowed to attend the general ***Darbar.***

Darbar takes decision on policy formulations, and discuss issues related to village development. The Headman decides even the types of activities required for which a ***Darbar*** is held. They generally execute government funds.

Sources of Funds:

They do not have specific inflow of regular funds. Often they get contribution from the villagers. Very meagre amount they get from village shops, hats etc. They are yet to receive funds from MDC, MLA or MP's scheme. At times they receive small fund from the state government to construct village link roads and for making footpaths. They get involved with the government projects as and when asked to. But their role is limited to supervision of the work, for which they get meager remuneration

They have only functional relation with the District Council, and this relation is mainly in terms of traditional matters like customary practices. But their relation with ***elaka Darbar or Sirdar Darbar*** is generally connected with serious matters, like disputes which are unsolved. He generally seeks advice from ***elaka Darbar*** to solve the matter.

Suggestions regarding changes in powers and functions of Darbar:

i. ***Darbar*** requires more power to develop strong defense for the people of the village.

ii. They should be given power to execute development work independently.

iii. They need power to integrate all the bodies of self-government.

iv. The term of Nongphoh village ***Darbar*** is only 3 years. But if the villagers are satisfied with their functioning, why cannot they be allowed to function for a term of 30-40 years, instead of having election every 3 years and spending money unnecessarily.

Case Study IV:

Wahiajer Village Headman under Jaintia Hills District:

There are total 6 localities in this village, out of which 5 are under Jowai ***Dolloi elaka*** and one under Nongbah ***Dolloi elaka***. But half of the forest areas under this village belong to Nortyang village. Each locality is comprised of one Secretary and one Chairman, who are also the members of the village ***Darbar (Darbar Shnong)***.

In the village ***Darbar*** there are 30-40 executive members. In the village court the accused are prosecuted in the process of administration of justice.

In the matter of land dispute, the headman is the supreme authority to take action with the consensus of the members of the ***Darbar***. The case, which is undecided, is referred to his ***elaka Dolloi***.

Women are not allowed, as a matter of principle, to participate in the ***Darbar***.

Any body other than women who wants to render voluntary service to the people of the village for their betterment are even welcome to become a member of the village ***Darbar***.

Several Improvement Functions of the Headman:

The village headman mobilises every household of his village to protect the forest from fire. Those households who do not cooperate in these activities are fined. Moreover if any person steals pine tree from the forest has to give fine to the ***Darbar***. If anyone is unable to pay the fine, he will be denied firewood and the wood required for burial until he pays the fine for his offence.

Government does involve the ***Darbar*** in their own project in their locality. But the headman is not satisfied with the work of District Council as well as Government, because they do not look after the interest of the village people or ***Darbar***. So far, in his 21 years of service, he has received funds for the following purposes from the MDC.

i. Drinking Water	= Rs. 10,000/-
ii. Foot-path construction	= Rs. 20,000/-
iii. Road making construction	= Rs. 80,000/-

The village resources (Paddy field and forest) are divided among the *elakas* mentioned below:

Paddy field	under ***Dolloi*** Nartiyang (a portion)
	Under ***Dolloi*** Nongbah (a minor portion)
Forest	under ***Dolloi*** Jowai (½ of the portion)
	Under ***Dolloi*** Nartiyang (½ of the portion)

The Headman's work is mainly supervisory and voluntary service. He is to take care of the welfare of the people of his village, and to check corruption. He has to look after other services too which includes supply of drinking water, making of footpath by organising the local people, and looking after the primary schools. Even if furniture is required for the primary schools he has to arrange woods and other equipment. However, for these purposes he mobilises funds from different sources like District Council, MDC, MLA or State Government.

As to the ***Dolloi,*** he says that they are the recommending authority in matters of land document like land ***patta,*** etc. The ***Dolloi*** also collects some land revenue especially from paddy field. For land ***patta*** they collect Rs.60/- per 8 kms. and for more than 8 km. Rs.80-85/- from the public. These rates are fixed at the District Council.

Generally they discuss the following issues in the village ***Darbar*** :

i. Land Disputes ii. Theft and Punishment. iii. Rules and Regulation of the Village.

The forest woods are distributed among the villagers. The table–2 below gives details:

Table–2
Distribution of Forest Wood among the Villagers

SN.	*Type(s) of wood*	*Purpose*	*No(s) allotted*	*One time/ More than one*
1.	Chyrngan Macalain (Jungle wood)	House making Use for plinth	5 5	One time One time
2.	Macalain "	Kitchen Cowshed	3 3	More than one time for extensive purposes
3.	"	Dead body	1 (for every dead body in a family)	More than one time
4.	Jungle wood (Rtiang)	For fire wood	4	Every winter
5.	Pine	For Furniture	Depending on the requirement	But one time only

Source: Information collected from the headman of the concerned village *Darbar.*

Everyone in the village gets woods according to his entitlement and needs, but not according to his greed. They have to use the wood for the purpose for which they collect and for which they have to procure receipt from the Secretary of the *Darbar.* The Secretary of the *Darbar* maintains record accordingly.

Entitlement lasts as long as he/she is in the village. If they leave the village and come back after a long time, they have to pay a fine of Rs.500/- as an entry fee.

6

Raid Council

Raid or *sub-raid* is a political unit comprising a number of adjacent Khasi villages organised into a political system for the purpose of social control and harmonious civil and judicial administration. This is the largest political unit under a state or ***Syiemship*** over which the Khasis wield political authority. The ***blang*** or ***sub-raid*** is smaller than the *raid;* it functions in a similar manner as the raid. There is a ***Durbar*** Raid at the ***raid*** level, which may be called territorial tribal council. In other words, it is commune comprising several villages with a commune ***Darbar*** or ***Raid Darbar*** at the top to manage its internal affairs. The ***Raiḍ Darbar*** is generally presided over by an elected headman (***Sirdar***) or priest (***Lyngdoh***). The ***Raid Darbar*** generally consists of one ***Lyngdoh*** and four ***Myntries***. The ***Myntries*** always act as councilor to the commune headman as well as to the chief of the state. The territorial tribal council settles the internal affairs, both civil and judicial. The ***Raid Darbar*** also settles boundary disputes between villages, looks after the land and forest within the *raid* and prevents unauthorised occupation and poaching. He is the custodian and implementing authority of the traditional law and custom. He is thus often called upon to discharge the duties of an arbitrator. The disputes, which cannot be settled at the raid level, are adjudicated by the ***Syiem's Darbar***, or by the chief. However, in the cases of serious crimes which involve life imprisonment and death sentences the territorial council has no power to take a decision. Such serious and complicated cases are to be referred to the chief. But presently such cases are to be referred to the District Council. The *Durbar raid* also approves and confirms the election of the officials of the commune, such as ***Lyngdohs, Myntries, Basan, Sirdars*** **and** ***Lynskors***. It is only after the approval of the ***Darbar Raid*** that the appointment of the officials is generally referred to the ***Syiem*** for his final assent.

The internal administration of each "Raid" or commune is run by an open ***Darbar*** where all male adults of the commune are invited by public announces by beating of drums, and every one present has equal rights of discussion and vote in the proceedings. In short democratic principle is scrupulously followed and all state matters are transacted after full deliberation in an open ***Darbar.***

Darbar summoned by the issue of private notices are not recognised and any resolution or orders passed by such ***Darbars*** are null and void. The notice for a ***Darbar*** must be public either through public announces by beating drums or by ***"Purwanas".***

In this regard we conducted two case studies in the East Khasi Hills District and the other in the Ribhoi District.

Case Study – I :

Raid Sardar **under Sohra** ***Syiemship*** **under East Khasi Hills**

Under this ***Raid,*** there are four villages with four clans namely, ***Dongskul, Ducanroad, Mawpun,*** and ***Pynshatkherai,*** which represent the ***Raid Darbar***. The four villages develop a commune, and bring all problems to the ***Raid Darbar*** to solve them. Generally they do not send the cases to the ***Syiem Darbar***. The *Darbar* consists of 18 members.

The ***Raid Sarda***r does not get salary; they render voluntary service for the welfare of the people. The people of these four villages elect ***raid Sardar,*** but the raid Sardar generally chooses the office bearers. After the candidate is elected, it has to be confirmed by the KHADC before he formally takes over the charge as ***raid Sardar***.

Relationship with *Syiem*

The ***Darbar Hima*** maintains a very cordial relation with the ***raids*** and ***Raid Sardar***.

Land Matter:

The ***Syiem*** does not intervene the in the land matter as the area is under the control of raid ***Sardar*** or village headman. If there is some dispute on ownership of land or other litigation, the matter is generally referred to ***Syiem Darbar*** via ***Raid Sardar***.

Administrative and Judicial Matters

In administrative and judicial matters the raid is subordinate to ***Syiem Darbar*** or ***Hima Darbar***. The raid is authorised to look after the development and protection of land through customary law. If a ***raid Sardar*** is unable to function accordingly, he cannot claim his position and right over his area.

The ***Syiem*** maintains law and order situation with the help of the ***raid Sardars, raid Darbar***, village headman and the village ***darbar***. Petty criminal cases are handled by the ***raid darbar***. The criminal may be fined or put in to their own jail but the serious cases are handed over to the police.

Source of income:

The source of income of the ***raid sardar*** is very limited. As he cannot raise any revenue from the villagers, he has to depend on the ***musur***, a sort of tax collected from the ***bazar*** falls under his jurisdiction. He gets some meager amount from MDCs to do some development work like footpath,link road construction etc. They are not involved in any government project directly.

There are only three types of land found under this ***Symship***:

i. ***Raid land*** – Land possessed by ***raid*** for the purpose of development. The management of the land is under the control of ***raid darbar.***

ii. ***Put*** land (***Ryknti***/Private) – land belonging to ***put*** i.e., to the private individual but no absolute ownership.

iii. Clan land – land possessed by respective clans.

Types of Forest Resources:

There are four kinds of forests :

i. Sacred Forest: People are not entitled to use this forest. Only after a gap of 15 years thinning process is carried out. In this process the poor and victimised people are benefited who get the old and dead trees. Other non-eligible people using this forest for any purpose are fined or penalised heavily.

ii. Village community forest (***Lawadong***) : Controlled and used at the dictation of village ***darbar***.

iii. Protected Forest (***Law Pyllait***): Protected by ***Hima***. Only leaves which falls during winter season are allowed to be taken away (one-person one head load) for fire or for domestic use but not for sale.

iv. Individual forest : (***Rykynti***) Forest belongs to the individuals. They can use the forest at their discretion.

Case Study–II :

Nongpoh Raid under Nongpoh (Re-Bhoi) Sardarship.

There are seven raids, namely i. ***Raid Nongpoh***; ii. ***Nongkrabi***; iii. ***Unsaumsaw – nongkharai***; iv. ***Nong Lyngdoh***; v. ***Nongakalta***; vi. ***Japro***; vii. ***Nongkhyllem***.

It has been learnt that these raids do not have good relation with their ***sardar***, as they feel that the status of their ***sardar*** is low as compared to the ***syiem***. Hence, all these raids function independently.

But they keep good relations with the ADC in matters of customary rights and traditions.

Raid heads are generally ***Lyungdoh,*** and they have to be from the same clan. A ***Raid*** consists of 7-8 ***members*** from ***different*** clans. For example, in ***raid darbar,*** the secretaries are from ***Synkly*** clan or ***lapang*** clan. These clans select the ***Basans*** who are the members of ***Darbar***. Electorates are also from the same clan. Members are also taken from ***Marie clan, lamalaies*** clan and ***Lyngdohsat*** clan. Priests are from the ***Lyngdohsat*** clan.

In the case of ***Nongpooh*** raid, the secretary acts as head of the ***raid*** in the absence of ***raid sardar.*** In the other raids under this ***sardarship,*** the members are having different titles and they are also taken from different clans. But the head of the raid is always from ***Lyngdoh*** clan.

Power of the raid *Sardar*

i. Full powers in regard to the land belonging to raid land. But not on individual land.

ii. Land documents (***dalil***) are issued by the ***raid sardar.*** Whenever any villager transfers his land to another tribal or legal heir, he/she has to report to the raid ***darbar. Raid*** members take decisions and ***the sardar raid*** issues patta. Raid land can be given on lease for 3 years, and in that case it is to be informed to District Council.

Raids can deal with two types of land documents.

(a) The land which can be transferred/sold/mortgages without the approval of competent authority.

(b) Land ***patta*** is issued only for three years.

Types of land

There are two types of land existing under this *Sardarship*—

(a) ***Raid land*** – any persons cannot occupy lands without the permission of ***raid Sardar.***

(b) ***Sacred land*** – are generally located in hillock, which is considered no man's land and traditionally the villagers perform ***puja*** on this sacred land. In Puja villagers generally sacrifice cocks which they believe would cure some critical diseases or suffering. But now-a-days most of the people become become Christians; hence the practice is no more there.

(c) ***Put*** land (***Khydaolajaong***) :

This land is allotted to the individual with the condition that it should be used for productive purposes. If it is not done within a time frame the land is taken back by the ***raid Sardar***.

Forest:

Raids, which see to it that there should not be any encroachment the forest, protect Forest by outsiders and the villagers as per the customary law use.

7

Conclusion with Recommendations

This study on 'Functioning of Autonomous District Council in Meghalaya', is based on facts and ground realities. The author took particular care to avoid any controversies as well as wrong information. The data generated were properly verified so that it can be an authentic write-up.

The study focuses on the existence and functioning of ADC in Meghalaya. The main purpose of the discussion was to find out the reason and justification of creation of Autonomous District Council in the State of Meghalaya. The very purpose of creating District Council was to protect the tribal people with their cultural heritage as well as their socio-economic life and living. But on the contrary the committee responsible for setting up such bodies failed to understand the sentiment of the local chiefs as a result of which the conflict between District Council, i.e. the functionaries of District Council and the Chiefs of the Twenty-Five Khasi States and non-states started. However, this is yet to take a violent form but internal non-cooperation is very much prevalent. Naturally, the District Council does not get sufficient cooperation from the chiefs although the chiefs have been given magisterial powers to function with limited capacity. But the chiefs feel that their major powers have been snatched away and they are not at all involved in development programmes of government. After attaining statehood, the District Council is standing alone with all its functions, powers and privileges. Further, the Khasi states and the Autonomous District Council are unable to maintain mutual cordial relation. To wither away District Council is not possible, as it is a statutory body under the provision of the constitution. On the other hand, the state has been created on the choice of the people of Meghalaya. But the Chiefs of the Khasi states and non-states claim their major stake. Whatever the reasons may be the Khasi states and non-states stand on their traditional values, wherein people feel more comfortable. Someone may have wrong conception about Khasi Chiefs; in fact they are neither autocrat nor feudal. They do not control the means of production of the people. People are allowed to possess any amount of land in their individual name. Customary laws framed by the people through consensus control all community land, clan land, forestland or sacred lands. The Chiefs are just titular heads who enjoy some tributes according to the desire of the local people. Hence, they are just custodians.

The situation, as such, is a very complex one. In order to find out the truth, several case studies were conducted at the Chiefs (Syiem, Lyngdoh, Sirdar, Wahadadar and Dolloi) level, Commune (raid) level as well as Darbar level. The system was found to be quite coherent and integral. The existing customary laws have no doubt bound the society to a self-content republic. What is important at this stage is to find out a solution to the problem of the inter – intra dispute and conflict. Instead of looking at the personal interest it would be wise to see the general interest which might benefit everyone. Constitutional provision for creating a statutory local govt. is no doubt very much important but at the same time it should adhere to the needs and aspirations of local people. If this is not done, then there may be anomaly in the society, and I am afraid, this might lead to destruction. However, the local government also faces some problems in its progress which are mentioned below:

Local self-government is the foundation of democracy. Now the question is whether we have made any progress in the right direction even after the creation of statutory local self-government in Meghalaya. Quantitatively, yes, there is some progress. Qualitatively there is absolute not.

1. The local authorities were entrusted with a variety of functions. Legislative, executive, and judicial. They were entrusted with some delegated functions. But most of them did not exercise all the functions entrusted to them. Particularly in regard to taxation the local authorities hesitated to take any action.

2. In Khasi Hills, the ***Syiems*** continued to function as independent rulers and realised revenues from markets, fines, from the administration of justice and occasional ceases levied for state purposes. They also received fifty percent of the rents realised from exploitation of the natural resources. The District Council did not exercise any control in regard to markets. Although there are many markets owned by the ***Syiems,*** the District Council received a very small amount from them.

3. The expenditure of District Councils was excessive on the establishment like the Meghalaya Secretariat.

4. Finally there was chronic political instability in the Khasi Hills. Leadership was changed very frequently.

In view of the above stated problems the following recommendations are made as remedial measures for better functioning of ADC:

1. The composition of local government was not completely democratic. They contained nominated members. The authority to nominate members was the Minister of Tribal Affairs. Very often he nominated persons who

would support the party in power. Sometimes nominations were made to enable a minority party to become a majority party and from the government. Sometime nominations were made to enable a person to become the CEM. There we think there is no need for nomination. It is suggested that all the members of a local authority must be elected.

2. Double membership – both in local authorities and the members parliament or legislative assembly. This is an undesirable provision. If an M.D.C. is also a member of parliament or the legislative assembly, he would draw salary in two places. It prevents some persons from participating in decision making. Double membership enables some persons to exercise influence on the government.

   If an M.D.C. is also a cabinet members, then he controls the District Council completely. Hence, double membership should be abolished. As in general cases the MLAs are not permitted to become members of parliament.

3. Qualifications and disqualifications for Members of District Council.

i. Residential qualification should be insisted upon.

ii. Members who failed to pay their dues in time should be disqualified.

iii. Members who interest themselves in a subsisting contract with a local authority should be disqualified from being members.

iv. Persons who had been removed by the government from membership should be disqualified from contesting elections within the prescribed period.

4. The District Council should enhance their capacity to implement Government sponsored programmes.

5. The ways should be found out in order to resolve the age long conflicts with the Khasi States.

6. General elections to the local authorities should be held at regular intervals like the Lok Sabha and Legislative Assembly. If the elections are not held at regular intervals, local authorities cease to be representative in character.

NOTES

1. The Khasi Chiefs formed Federation of Khasi states in 1956 with the following objectives:
   i. To preserve the rights and customs of the Khasi people;
   ii. to act as an intermediary body between Khasi states and the Government;
   iii. to act as a Supreme Court of appeal for the Khasi in the country;
   iv. to assume legitimate control of affairs relating to the Khasi states;
   v. To establish independent relationships between the Khasi states and the princely states of India; to demand higher judicial powers and autonomous bodies.

2. The nineteen states which signed the Instrument of Accession are–

   1. Khyrim 2. Mylliem 3. Cherra 4. Nongkhlaw 5. Bhowal 6. Jirang 7. Maharam 8.Mawsynram 9. Langrin 10. Mawiang 11. Malaisohmat 12. Mawphang 13. Lyniong 14.Sohiong 15. Shella 16. Nonglwai 17. Pamsanagnt 18. Mawdon and 19. Dwara Nongtyrmen.

   The six states, which signed later on, are –

   1. Nobosohphoh 2. Nongspung 3. Mawlong 4. Rambrai 5. Myriaw 6. Nongstoin

3. The recommendations of the Bordoloi Committee are as follows:
   i. The Tribal System should be kept intact till the tribal people change their way of life.
   ii. There should be control of immigration and that there should be no allocation of land to outsiders. The district council should have power of legislation over the occupation, setting apart and use of land other than land comprising reserved forests. The actual management of forests, other than reserved forests, including the appointment of forest staff and the granting of leases and contract should be according to the need and desire of the people.

iii. The mode of cultivation of land should be left to the tribes themselves. Jhuming was to be discouraged and stopped whenever possible; no legislative ban was to be imposed without the consent of the tribesmen. Control of jhuming was to be left to the district council.

iv. The District Councils were to have full powers of administering their own social laws, of codifying or modifying them.

v. The District Councils should manage primary schools, dispensaries and such other institutions. District Councils might be permitted to manage secondary schools but not the higher education.

vi. District Councils should be vested with legislative power over the use of land, village forests, agriculture, and village and town management in addition to the administration of tribal and local laws.

vii. There should be allocation of certain taxes and financial powers to the District Councils.

viii. Any District Council might, by three-fourth majority introduce the system of licensing of moneylenders and traders.

ix. No license or lease regarding the management of minerals and mines shall be granted without consulting with the District Council.

x. No provincial or central law should be applied to Hill Areas without the consent of the District Councils concerned.

xi. If any Autonomous District was inhabited by more than one tribe, the Regional council should be established.

xii. The Governor should have the power to dissolve any District Council when and if necessary.

xiii. Hill areas should be represented in the Assam Legislative on the basis of adult francise.

xiv. Adequate tribal representatives should be there in both Provincial and Central Legislatures.

xv. The Hill areas should be represented in the Assam Cabinet by at least one of the Hill members and there should be a special Minister from among the Hill MLAs.

xvi. There was a need for review of the development work periodically by a commission to be appointed by the Governor.

xvii. Non-tribals should not have the right to contest the elections to the provincial and Central Legislatures. But they might be represented in the District Councils.

4. The following Six Tribal districts of Assam were included as Autonomous Districts under the Sixth Schedule of the Constitution of India, 1950 :

i. The United Khasi – Jaintia Hills District

ii. The Garo Hills District (now Mizoram)

iii. The Naga Hills District

iv. The North Cachar Hills District

v. The Mikir Hills District

A District Council is authorised to enact laws with respect to the allotment and use of land other than land under reserved forests, canal and watercourse, regulation of shifting cultivation, establishment of village or town committees. Further, the District council is authorised to make appointment or succession of Chiefs or Headmen, inheritance of property, marriage and divorce, etc. All laws passed by the District Council shall have no effect until assented to by the Governor. It has also the power to assess and collect land revenue and to impose taxes on professions, trades, callings and employment,

Animals, vehicles and boats, the entry of goods into a market for sale, tolls on passengers and goods etc. The District Councils shall have share of licenses or leases for the purpose of prospecting for, or extraction of minerals granted by the state government in respect of any area falling within the autonomous district concerned. It has the power of regulating and controlling money lending and trading by non-tribal within the district.

The council enjoys the powers of establishing and managing primary schools, dispensaries, markets, cattle pound, ferries, fisheries, roads, road transport and waterways. It can prescribe the language and the manner in which education should be imparted in primary schools within its area.

It also enjoys, subject to the jurisdiction of the High Court, certain judicial powers –both civil and criminal – as the Governor may specify from time to time.

Even after the constitution of separate tribal states/union territories the autonomous tribal districts under the District Councils were retained. In case of Lusai (later called Mizoram) Hill District there were three autonomous regions, namely the Chakma, the Lakher and the Powi Autonomous regions. They are constituted as Autonomous District Councils.

At the time of the reorganization of the northeastern states, the following District Councils were constituted:

Assam :	**Meghalaya :**	**Mizoram :**
The North Cachar Hills	Khasi Hills District	The Chakma District
The Mikir Hills (now	Jaintia Hills District	The Lakher District
(Karbi Anglong)	Garo Hills District	The Powi District

References

Appointment of succession of Chiefs Act, 1959.

Administrative Report of Khasi and Jaintia Hills, 1875-76.

Bose, Manilal, "Historical and Constitutional Documents of North-East India" (1824-1973). Delhi, Concept Publishing Company, 1979, pp. 182-184.

Bareh, H. *History and Culture of the Khasi People*, Passim, nd.

_________, *Khasi Democracy*, 1964, pp. 37–38.

Bhattacharya, U. '*Syiemships*', in Chattopadhyay (ed.), *Tribal Institution of Meghalaya*, Guwahati, Spectrum Publications, 1985, P.52.

Constitution Assembly Debate, Vol.9, p. 1008.

Cajee, Chief Executive Members vs. C. Jormanik Syiem and another, C.A. 394, 1960 (S.C.)

District Council's report to Vaghaiwalla Committee, 1959-60, p.27.

District Council has abolished revenue on *raj hali lands.*

Dutta, Sujit, K. 'Autonomous Local Government in NE States : A Function Analysis' in Fifty Years of Rural Development in India: Retrospect and Prospect, ed. by R.C. Choudhury, S. Rajakutty, July 1998, p.58.

Ganguly, J.B., 'Role of Autonomous District Council in Meeting Tribal Aspirations for Development in Tripura', in Madhu S. Mishra ed *Rural Development in Eastern and North – Eastern India,* Indian Institute of Management, Calcutta, 1988.

Gassah, L.H. 'Village Administration in Jaintia Hills', paper presented in a seminar on the Indigenous Institutions of Garos, The Khasis and the Jaintia Hills of Meghalaya, Shillong, 1980.

Gordon, PRT, *The Khasis,* a paper presented in a seminar on ' Social and Political Institutions of the Hill People of NE India, Shillong, 1907, pp 66-75.

_________, *The Khasis,*(Reprint), London, 1914, P.75.

Information collected from JHADC, 2000

Instrumentation of Accession of Khasi Hills States, August 7, 1948.

Jyrwa, E. 'Financial Status of Local Institutions in the Khasi and Jaintia Hills Autonomous District of Meghalaya', unpublished document, n.d.

Kharlukhis, B.R., Administration of Justice in the Khasi Hills, in Chattapadhyay (ed.), *Tribal Institutions of Meghalaya,* Guwahati; Spectrum publications, 1985, pp. 115-116.

Letter of the Chairman Constitution – Making Darbar of the Khasi States to the Governor of Assam (for excluded Area and States), Shillong, dated the 25th October 1949.

Lyngdoh R.S. *Government and Politics in Meghalaya.* New Delhi, Sanchar Publishing House, 1996, p.25.

Mathur, P.R.G., *The Khasi of Meghalaya,* New Delhi, Cosmo Publications, 1979, P.67.

Menon, V.P., *Integration of Indian States,* New Delhi, Orient Longman, 1997, pp. 310-311.

Phira, J.M. *Public Administration in Meghalaya,* Shillong, Tech – quip, 1996, P.90.

Pugh, B. *The Khasis of Assam,* n.d., p. 32

Roy, David. In *Cantle's Notes on Khasi Law,* Reprint, 1994, pp. 116–117.

Rymbai, R.T. *The Evolution of the Hynnietrep Polity,* ed. by U. Sumar Singh Sawian, *Khansmari – Ukhun Uhajar Ka Rl Hynniewtrep,* Shillong, Apphish Publications, 1998.

Syiem, Baljied, 'Syiemships district councils can't co-exist', covered by the ***Grass-roots voices,*** October 26 – November 1, 1988.

Shullai, L.F , *Ba Ioh Ngi Klet (pt.I),* November 23, 1964. P.6.

Singh, Kynpham, 'Syiems and Darbars in Khasi Polity', in *Tribal Institutions of Meghalaya* (ed.) by Chattopadhyay, S.K. Shillong, 1985, pp. 1–8.

APPENDIX – I

Statement shows Constituencies within the Jaintia Hills District Council

1. Jowai North	Parts of Jowai and Nongbah Dolloiships.
2. Jowai South	Parts of Jowai and Amwi Dolloiships.
3. Wahiajer	Parts of Jowai, Nongbah and Nartiang Dolloiship
4. Nongbah–Nongjngi–Mynso	Parts of Nongbah, Mynso, Nongjngi and Shangpung Dolloiships.
5. Nartiang	Rest of Nartiang Dolloiships.
6. Shiliang–Myntang	Parts of Shiliang–Myntang and Nongjngi Dolloiships.
7. Raliang	Part of Raliang Dolloiships.
8. Mookaiaw	Rest of Raliang Dolloiships.
9. Shangpung	Parts of Shangpung and Sutnga Dolloiships.
10. Tuber	Parts of Jowai and Shangpung Dolloiships.
11. Sutnga–Sumer–Nongkhlieh	Parts of Sutnga and Nongkhlieh Dolloiships.
12. Saipung	Parts of Saipung Sirdarship and Sutnga Dolloiships.
13. Rymbai-Narpuh	Parts of Rymbai, Sutnga and Narpuh Dolloiships.
14. Rangad–Lakadong	Parts of Rymbai and Jowai Dolloiships and Lakadong Elaka.
15. War Jaintia (East)	Parts of Nongtalang and Satpator Dolloiships.
16. War Jaintia (West)	Parts of Darang, Nongtalang, Jowai and Amwi Dolloiships.

Vide Government Notification No.DCA. 119/77/62 dated 6th May 1978.

APPENDIX - II

Electoral Constituencies in The Hills of Autonomous District Council, as in October 1983

1. Nartiang - Wahiajer	12. Sutnga
2. Modop - Khanduli	13. Narpuh
3. Nongjngi	14. Rymbai - Khliehriat
4. Tangrain - Barato	15. Rangad - Lakadong
5. Mookaiaw	16. Musniang - Mustem
6. Laskein - Iooksi	17. Tuber - Bapung
7. Shangpung	18. Jowai (North)
8. Mynso - Raliang	19. Jowai(Central)
9. Nongbah	20. Jowai(South)
10. Sumer - Jalaphet	21. War (West)
11. Saipung	22. War (East)

Vide Gazette of Meghalaya (Extraordinary) No.112 dated 9th November 1983.